CW00394775

EASIER RIGS FOR SAFER CRUISING
Sailhandling from the Cockpit

Easier Rigs
For Safer Cruising

Sailhandling from the Cockpit

John Campbell

HOLLIS & CARTER

LONDON

British Library Cataloguing
in Publication Data
Campbell, John
Easier rigs for safer cruising : sailhandling
from the cockpit.
1. Masts and rigging   2. Sailboats
I. Title
623.8'62   VM531
ISBN 0–370–30698–8 paperback

© John Campbell 1986
Photoset in Baskerville and printed in Great Britain for
Hollis & Carter
an associate company of
The Bodley Head Ltd
30 Bedford Square, London WC1B 3RP
by Redwood Burn Limited, Trowbridge, Wiltshire
First published 1986

CONTENTS

The photographs are supplied
by the author.

The line illustrations are drawn
by Linda McFie and Geoff Page.

The photograph numbered 1 is the author's; the
photograph numbered 2 is supplied by courtesy of
Newbridge Boats Ltd/Crescent Studios; those
numbered 31 and 41, by courtesy of Sunbird Yachts Ltd
(the former taken by Alastair Black);
those numbered 42 and 43, by courtesy of
Mr J. Manners-Spencer; those numbered 48, 49 and 59,
by courtesy of Freedom Yachts International; and
the photograph numbered 55, by courtesy of
Gougeon Brothers, Inc.

I

Let's Stay off the Foredeck!

Like many other cruising people, my wife Lana and I usually sail with just the two of us on board. We are not interested in sailing with a large crew, who would perhaps help us get there a little faster; we prefer our own company, and our own pace. We do not mind taking a little longer, provided that we can complete the passage in safety and reasonable comfort. Current yacht design seems to be concentrating more and more on heavily crewed ocean racers, with scarcely a thought for the likes of us, or for the small cruiser sailed by the family, which in practice is often sailed singlehanded by Dad, while Mum tends to the children. It is our intention here to look at ways of making life easier and safer for crews sailing shorthanded.

The most serious danger that we face when cruising on a sailing boat is falling overboard. This risk is probably at its greatest when we are on a pitching foredeck, perhaps during a dark and windy night, wrestling with a flapping sail that needs to come down. People persist in working on deck when it is possible to arrange all sailhandling to be done from the safety of the cockpit. When all the sails can be easily handled without anybody going on deck, the crew are less likely to get wet and tired, or fall overboard, and more likely to enjoy themselves. We are supposed to go sailing for pleasure!

The moment one leaves the cockpit to go on deck, the risk of falling overboard is greatly increased, and once over the side, the chances of recovery are frighteningly small. One only has to reflect for a moment on the sad loss of Rob

James, who went over the side in only moderate conditions while stowing the mainsail on his large trimaran, to appreciate the dangers.

Here was a very experienced sailor, only a few miles from home, dropping the mainsail to slow down the boat until dawn. The crew were also very experienced, young and fit, and although they knew almost at once that he had gone, they were unable to recover him. If a strong experienced racing crew cannot recover a person in moderate conditions, what chance do Mother and the children have of rescuing Father if he goes off the foredeck when the wind pipes up a bit?

Every sailor recognises the value of a harness, and many will wear one most of the time, but who amongst us has never made a quick dash to the foredeck without hooking on, or having gone forward, has never unhooked just for a moment to reach a little bit farther than the harness will allow? I do not think that I am in the minority when I confess to having done both of these things several times.

All too often the family crew caught out in deteriorating conditions face the big dilemma. It is raining, getting dark and coming on to blow. Mother refuses to go up on the foredeck to drop the Number One jib, yet neither does she really want to steer while the Old Man goes up to do the job. She is cold, wet and apprehensive, and she really does not want him to be out of sight up there on the foredeck. But the jib still has to come down.

Maybe an argument ensues, and Father leaves the helm to make a quick dash forward to drop the jib. In his haste he doesn't hook on and at that moment a bigger wave than usual makes the over-canvassed boat broach. . . .

At worst, Father is lost over the side, leaving his wife and children to try and recover him. At the very best, Mother decides that next weekend the gardening club has a meeting that she cannot miss; she prefers not to go sailing, just to avoid the risk of a repeat performance.

One piece of equipment that might well help in this type of situation would be some form of self steering. This used to be considered as gear required only for transocean passages, yet some form of self steering can make life so much easier aboard any boat, even one undertaking only modest coastal passages. The small electronic types are now quite reasonable in cost, and use little power, yet if they can release the helmsman from his station in time of crisis, or just let him put the kettle on or take a bearing, they can be worth their weight in gold, or at least worth another crew member. If the budget just will not run to such a device, then it is a good idea to devise some quick and easy way of securing the helm, so the boat can sail herself at least for a few minutes.

In the sailing magazines we regularly read about the best way to recover a person from the water, and indeed this is a very important subject in itself. We also keep being reminded about the importance of wearing a harness, and there is no doubt that this adds greatly to one's safety, especially if it is used with the remarkable 'Latchway' system. This is a device that allows the harness tether to move along the jack-stay, and actually bypass support brackets without being unhooked. It is very dangerous to unhook the tether even momentarily to pass an obstruction or support. If a 'Latch-way' is not used, there should be two clips on the tether, so that when passing an obstruction there will be one hook attached all the time.

These articles all imply that it is somehow inevitable that people are going to go over the side. Maybe it is time that we adopted a more positive approach, and looked at ways to reduce this risk, and the obvious way is to keep people in the cockpit, or down below, while we are sailing.

We have the technology to land people on the moon, yet when somebody down here on Mother Earth wants to make a passage under sail, he must regularly expose himself to the

1. Choppy conditions, but the crew of this unstayed cowhorn schooner *Sea Legs* can control each sail from the cockpit.

considerable danger of working on the open deck. How much safer, and—dare I say it?—more enjoyable the whole thing would be if we never had to leave the safety of the cockpit while sailing.

The usual reason for going onto the foredeck is to change sails. As the strength of the wind varies, most boats must change their sail area to suit, if they are to continue sailing efficiently. The force of the wind is proportional to the square of its speed, which means that there is a much greater change in force from ten to twenty knots, than there is from twenty to thirty knots. (Ten squared is one hundred, and twenty squared is four hundred, so the force on the sails has increased by four times for that ten-knot increase in wind speed. Thirty squared is nine hundred, so for an additional ten-knot increase in speed the force has little more than doubled.)

From this it follows that a change in sail area is more likely to be required in the lower wind speeds than in the higher ones. Once the wind is above about thirty knots, it will take quite a large change in wind speed to alter greatly the force on the sails. Thus, the wind speeds where we need the greatest flexibility in sail area are around ten to twenty-five knots. Outside this range, it is nice to have some provision for very light-weather sailing and, to be prudent, we should also be prepared for the winds of thirty knots and over.

The problem is not new. Ever since boats have been sailing, they have had to be able to change their sail area to suit the conditions. For many commercial vessels, the provision of a large crew was not economically viable, so ways were devised for small crews to handle large amounts of sail.

The Thames barges that still traded under sail commercially until the middle of this century are a good example. Many of these sailing barges displaced well over a hundred tons when laden, yet traditionally they were sailed on coastal passages by a man, a boy and a dog! Their answer to the sail-handling problem was to use small headsails and a small mizzen, to help balance the rig, with the bulk of the sail area being in an enormous mainsail, which was usually rigged with a sprit. A sail rigged in this way can usually be left hoisted. Instead of lowering the sail, it is brailed up to the mast, rather like gathering a stage curtain to one side in the theatre. Being able to do this saved having to raise the heavy sail each time. In fair weather, the barges could set a large topsail, and just lowering this not only reduced the sail area when the wind piped up, but it also lowered the Centre of Effort of the sail plan.

Another type of boat that was often sailed shorthanded was the pilot vessel. Often these boats would sail out to their station with several pilots aboard, but once the pilots were working, the vessel might be left with just the skipper and cook aboard. Off the coasts of Europe, these boats were often rigged as gaff cutters. Again, they had small headsails and a big mainsail whose area could be increased with the addition of a topsail. If the weather got bad, the jib could be lowered and the boat handled under staysail and reefed main. No sails had to be changed, only raised, lowered or reefed.

The American pilot vessels tended to be gaff schooners, but their rig evolved along quite similar lines. They had gaff main and foresails, either or both of which could have topsails set over them, and usually two small headsails.

The big old squareriggers had their sail area split into many small sails, and they changed the total area by taking in or setting some of the individual sails. It was not uncommon for such a vessel to have twenty-five or thirty sails, so the total area could be quite precisely controlled. Each individual sail was quite small in area, so that few people were needed to set, reef or furl it. Once brace winches were developed so that a small crew could brace the yards around when tacking, even the biggest squarerigged ships reduced their crew to as few as fifteen or eighteen in the latter days, when they were trying to compete economically with steam.

A modern racing sloop often possesses about the same number of sails, but of course, they are not all set at once, but are of varying sizes, to suit a narrow set of wind conditions. All these sails, and the constant sail changes, require large numbers of crew. It is not uncommon to see a forty-foot racing boat with twelve or more crew, and a seventy-foot maxi requires about twenty-five people to sail her at her best.

Many cruising boats have followed in the wake of their glamorous racing cousins without stopping to question if that is the best way. First of all, if a cruising boat carries half a dozen headsails, there is the expense of buying them all. Then, once on the boat, they all have to be stowed, even when they are well and truly wet and salty. Finally, when the time comes to change them, somebody has to be out there on the deck working with them. The vessels that managed to sail with small crews in the days of commercial sail all changed their sail area by raising, furling or reefing sails, never by substituting one sail for another of a different size.

Lana and I got the message several years ago when we delivered one of the OSTAR singlehanded boats back to England from Newport after the race. Despite supposedly being equipped for singlehanded sailing, she had, as I recall, nine headsails which, when bundled up in their bags, took up a disproportionate amount of the thirty-eight feet of boat. One of the first jobs we did, when getting the boat ready, was to take all those sails ashore, and fold them up neatly. Since we were not in a hurry, and were looking forward to an easy and hopefully gentle passage back to England, I decided that some of the sails could be packed away as 'not wanted on the voyage'. We would leave the very light sails folded up neatly, and start off with the Number Two genoa bent on. If we got a stronger breeze, then the working jib would suffice, with the storm jib handy for any ugly weather.

Unfortunately it was not to be. We soon found that the boat was a little tender, and if she was the slightest bit over-pressed she just lay down on her ear and wallowed. When she had just the right amount of sail up she went very well, seven knots hour after hour, but let the wind ease just a little, then her performance dropped dramatically, and she begged for more sail. Despite trying not to, we ended up using every sail on the boat except the storm jib, and logged over forty sail changes between Newport and the Azores, on what was essentially a gentle cruise. We got most of the sails wet, and once they were bundled into the forward cabin,

2. Junk-rigged 21-foot Coromandel by Newbridge Boats: sailhandling without tears.

they took up almost one third of the room below, and the dampness that they exuded spread through the rest of the boat.

I had been toying with the idea of a junk-rigged boat for several years, and that passage made up my mind. Our next boat would do away with all this nonsense—we would have a boat where the sails could be easily reefed for changing conditions, with no more 2 a.m. visits to the foredeck in the rain to change sails, and no more wet sails to be dragged down below.

*   *   *

There are several ways that sails can be reefed. They can be folded up along the foot, or they can be rolled up along either the foot or the luff. A variety of systems have evolved, some being easier to use than others, and some allowing the reefed sail to set better than others. There are very sophisticated systems that are often quite expensive, but there are also some very simple and cheap alternatives. We will look at a selection of these systems, and compare cost and reliability —and find that one is not necessarily a function of the other.

We will look first at how it is possible to arrange a conventional sloop to allow all or most sailhandling to be done from the cockpit. For quite a modest outlay we can avoid most of the unpleasantness and danger of working on the foredeck.

From there we will look at how various other rigs, such as the Chinese junk and the cat rigs, have developed. Some of these rigs, most notably the junk, offer incredibly easy reefing. Along the way we will discover the joy of sailing with a self-tending rig. With such a rig, there is usually no headsail, so there are no headsail sheets to winch in after every tack. That can really make short tacking a pleasure.

We will endeavour to point out some of the many choices of reefing systems and rigs that are now available, and try to help the reader evaluate just what is the best choice for him. We will look at how lightweather sails and spinnakers can be handled with ease and safety, and also examine how the modern unstayed mast, which is at the heart of many of these alternative rigs, is made.

Hopefully more people will be encouraged to sail from the safety of the cockpit, and perhaps they will find that they enjoy sailing even more, when they discover just how easy it can be. Remember, we are supposed to go sailing because it is fun.

2

Taming the Mainsail
A look at various reefing systems for the mainsail

There are really two basic systems for reefing the mainsail. We can use some form of slab reefing, where the area of the sail is reduced by folding up the lower portion and tying it out of the way, or we can reef it by partially rolling it up, along either the foot or the luff. Let's look at each system in turn, and see which is the easiest in practice, and also see how each system can be adapted to enable the reef to be put in without leaving the safety of the cockpit. We will try and remember some ideas that the old working sailors used, which many of the current sailors seem to have forgotten, and also look at some of the innovative ideas that are being developed.

Slab Reefing

Slab reefing is the most common way to reef the mainsail. The usual system involves first taking the weight of the boom on the topping lift. The halyard is partially lowered until a cringle on the luff can be slipped over a hook at the forward end of the boom. The halyard is re-tightened, and the cringle in the leech is pulled down to the boom using the reefing pendant. This is a line that runs out along the boom, round a cheek block, up through a cringle in the leech, and back down to the boom.

It's much easier to pull the leech cringle down to the boom if the sail is not full of wind. To put in a reef successfully, the boat must be at least beam-on, or pointing closer to the wind, with the sheet eased out. It is almost impossible to reef down on a dead run, or indeed to shake out a reef on such a course. The sail will be pressed hard against the shrouds, making it difficult to raise or lower it at all.

As soon as the leech cringle is pulled down to the boom, and the reefing pendant is secured, the sheet can be hardened in to stop the sail flogging, and the boat can be allowed to continue sailing.

To neaten the job, and to stop the reefed portion of the sail from flapping about, this loose bit of sail is usually rolled up to lie along the boom, and secured there using the reef points. If the boom has a track along it, and the sail is attached by slides, then the reef points should be passed under the boltrope of the sail, rather than around the boom itself. By tying the reef points under the boltrope, the stress is more evenly spread into the sail, and the reef points are less likely to tear the sail. It is also much easier to make the rolled up bundle of sail neater and less likely to be shaken loose by the wind when it is done this way rather than by tying the points under the boom. However, if the sail is set on the boom by means of a boltrope which fits into an integral groove in the boom, then there is no choice—the reef points must pass around the boom.

Incidentally, the proper knot to use for the job is the reef knot, otherwise known as the square knot. This is a knot that

3. Sail showing reefing pendant, reef points and luff cringle.

Reef Knot

4. Same sail reefed—showing reefing pendant pulled tight, reef points tied under the boltrope, luff cringle engaged in hook. Inset showing reef knot.

holds well, but can easily be untied by pushing the two tails into the knot.

We have often sailed on boats that have all the reefing controls terminating at the mast. This means that to put in a reef, at the very best, you have to make a round trip between the cockpit and the mast. You have to work up there on the plunging deck, often in the dark. The sail is usually flapping about wildly, and to tie in the reef points you need to reach up for the swinging boom, the end of which is sometimes far outboard. Why, when it is so easy to improve the arrangement? It is usually no problem to lead the tail of the reefing pendant back to the cockpit, and a similar pendant can be led through the luff cringle to pull it down. If the halyard is also led back to the cockpit, it is possible to tie in the basic reef without setting foot on deck.

With such an arrangement, the actions for taking in a reef are more or less the same as before. The sail is allowed to feather and the halyard is slackened away. The luff reefing pendant is pulled tight and secured, the halyard is re-tightened, leaving just the leech pendant to be pulled tight, and the reef is basically in, without anyone leaving the cockpit.

5. Sail with separate luff and leech reefing pendants which, together with the halyard, lead to the cockpit.

We have found that the whole procedure goes much more smoothly if the halyard is marked for the position of each reef, then just the right amount of halyard can be slackened off. If there is not enough slack, the luff pendant cannot be tightened properly, and too much slack may lead to a snarl-up, or problems when having partially to rehoist the sail after the pendant is tight.

If the reef points are not tied in, there will be a tendency for the loose part of the sail to flap about. It will probably not come to too much harm, but it will be annoying, to say the least. Rather than venturing on deck to roll up the flapping sail, and then struggling to tie in all the reef points, why not consider going the whole hog, and fit lazy jacks which will restrain the reefed portion of the sail?

Lazy jacks were much in evidence in the days of working sail. Large and unwieldy vessels, often with heavy gaff mainsails, were sailed in all kinds of weather, usually with very few crew. Many of the pilot cutters, and a lot of the larger fishing boats were fitted with lazy jacks on the mainsail, to help to control these big sails while they were being raised, lowered or reefed.

In their simplest form, lazy jacks are just loops of rope that pass under the boom and are suspended from the topping lift, or from a pair of topping lifts. Where they pass under the boom, they usually go through a lacing eye, or similar, so that they cannot move fore and aft along the boom. When the sail is lowered or reefed, it will fall between the lazy jacks, and it will tend to concertina on top of the boom. The lazy jacks will more or less hold the loose portion of the sail in place, or at least restrain it from flapping about. In practice, one loop of the lazy jack about every four feet or so along the boom will suffice.

There are many ways that the lazy jacks can be rigged. Loops can be hung from the existing single topping lift, but this can lead to chafe, particularly along the leech of the sail.

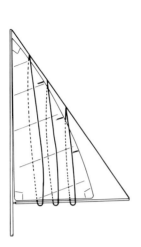
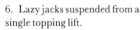

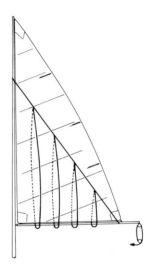

6. Lazy jacks suspended from a single topping lift.

7. Better system—lazy jacks suspended from a pair of topping lifts which are fitted about two thirds of the way up the mast.

A somewhat better way to rig them is to run two topping lifts from a point about two thirds of the way up the mast. The loops are hung between the two, and this reduces the amount of rope used, and removes the lazy jacks from the leech of the sail, where they are most likely to cause chafe.

The best device that we have used is one that more closely copies the Chinese system, and we will see variations on this theme when we look at the junk rig in detail. Again a pair of topping lifts are used, and they too are attached about two thirds of the way up the mast. In this case, though, the lifts themselves are quite short. From the end of each lift, a series of lazy jacks pass under the boom. This arrangement still further reduces the amount of rope used, and keeps the lazy jacks even further away from the leech of the sail.

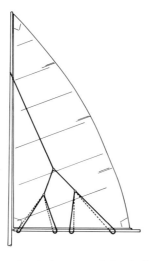

8. Best system—lazy jacks patterned after the Chinese style.

Whichever system is used, it will take some experimenting to get the length of each lazy jack just right. They have to be tight enough to restrain the sail, but not so tight that they press into the sail when sailing close-hauled.

We have found that in most cases it is better to retain the original topping lift which runs to the end of the boom when using lazy jacks. This allows the lazy jacks to be a little slack when the sail is being hoisted, which reduces the chance of the headboard or the leech fouling them. On a small boat, with a light boom, it would be worth experimenting to see how the lazy jacks performed without the main topping lift in place. It will not be needed on very small sails.

One easy way to make each loop in the system adjustable is to bring down one line from its topping lift, pass it through the lacing eye beneath the boom, and up for a couple of feet, before finishing it with an eye splice. The corresponding line on the other side is brought down and cut off a foot or so past where it meets the eye splice. The end is whipped and simply tied into the eye splice. Each loop of the device can now be easily adjusted from deck level.

We fitted lazy jacks to a sixty-foot schooner that we have been sailing in charter service. While it didn't make her as easy to sail as our junk-rigged boat, it certainly made the sails much easier to handle, not only when reefing, but also when dropping them. Now there is no danger that they will engulf the helmsman, nor obstruct his view at the crucial moment. As they drop, they more or less flake themselves down on top of the boom, and once the anchor is down, either Lana or myself can easily tidy up the stow, and flake them neatly on top of the boom. Before, it was an all-hands-on-deck job to get them stowed even half-way decently.

To return to the reefing system proper, it will be obvious that with this sytem two reefing pendants are needed for each reef, and so if we want to be able to put in two reefs, four pendants will be needed. This may look like a lot of ropes coming into the cockpit, but if they are colour-coded, or better still, led through marked fairleads or stoppers, it should not be a problem. Indeed, it is probably best to lead the lines through stoppers anyway, so that one winch can be used to tighten all four pendants in turn.

For those who are daunted by large numbers of ropes, there is a way of rigging this type of reefing system where one pendant will suffice for each reef. To do this, the reefing pendant is led from the cockpit to the base of the mast and up to the gooseneck as before. From there it passes between the sheaves of a sister block that is attached to the side of the boom near the gooseneck, and runs up the luff of the sail, through a block attached to the luff cringle and back down through a cheek block on the boom. It continues along the

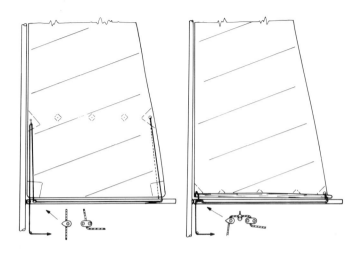

9. Sail fitted with continuous reefing pendant.

10. Sail with continuous reefing pendant reefed down.

boom as the reefing pendant did in the original system, to go through the leech cringle.

As the halyard is slackened away, and the reefing pendant pulled in, the block on the luff of the sail is pulled down until it lies against the boom, between the sister block and the cheek block. As the pendant is further tightened the leech cringle is pulled down. Once the cringle is pulled down to the boom, and the pendant secured, the halyard can be re-tightened as before.

We have sailed on only one boat that had this type of reefing arrangement, but it performed extremely well. It was also fitted with lazy jacks and we were able to reef and unreef quite happily from the cockpit, having to handle only the reefing pendant and the halyard. It worked just about as

23

11. Reefing pendant pulling at correct angle — almost parallel to the leech.

easily as on our own junk-rigged boat, except that we have the option of putting as many as five reefs in each of our sails.

Another pendant can be fitted on the other side of the boom for a second reef. It is not really feasible to use this system for more than two reefs, as it becomes impossible to get a fair lead for three pendants, so good deep reefs should be allowed for. While cruising I always feel that, if you have to reef, it is worth taking in a good-sized reef, otherwise you are likely to be taking in another one soon after. If one is prepared to accept the limitations of a two-reef sail, this method works well.

The secret of getting the sail to set well when reefed is largely a case of positioning the cheek block for the leech reefing pendant in the right place. They should be sited just an inch or two aft of where the leech cringle will be when it is pulled down to the boom. This is to put tension on the part of the sail that is now acting as the foot, which will help to keep the sail flat. If the block is positioned too far forward, the new foot will not be stretched out tight, the sail will belly out and be far too full for the windy conditions. If the block is positioned too far aft, it will be difficult to pull the cringle down to the boom. Just trying to pull the clew down, unnecessary loads will be placed on the reefing pendant. The

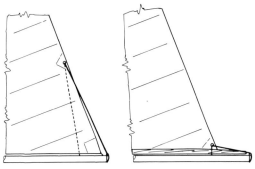

12. Reefing system to be avoided—pendant emerging from end of boom exerts an oblique pull when the sail is reefed down.

pendant will be under least load if it is working directly against the pull of the sail rather than at an angle to it. Most of the stress on the clew is along the line of the leech, particularly when the sail is sheeted in hard to go to windward. The cheek block for each reef should be positioned so that the direction of pull exerted by the pendant is almost parallel to the leech, with the new foot of the sail stretched out tight.

It has become somewhat trendy to copy the racers and lead all the reefing pendants inside the boom. This is fine, except that all too often you see the reefing pendant leading from the leech cringle to a sheave incorporated into the end-fitting of the boom. Such a system looks very streamlined, but can often be the cause of a poor set to the sail when reefed. Particularly when the second reef is being pulled down, the leech cringle can be far from the end of the boom; this results in an oblique pull which, we have already seen, increases the already considerable load on the pendant. Often the end of the pendant is fastened to the boom near the leech cringle to try and minimise the effect of the oblique pull. Unfortunately this causes the pendant to exert a twisting force on the leech cringle, which puts an added stress on the clew of the sail, and could well cause chafe on the pendant itself.

We recently delivered a much advertised and quite successful thirty-nine foot cruiser-racer that had just this solution for reefing. By the time the second reef was down, the leech cringle was about four or five feet forward of the end of the boom, where the reefing pendant emerged. Despite using the mast-mounted reefing winch to tighten the pendant, we could not get it tight enough to keep the leech cringle close to the boom once the sail was sheeted in. The sail set rather poorly, and after only five or six hours of sailing with the mainsail reefed, the pendant was already quite badly chafed because of the high tension and the oblique pull.

Such a system is perhaps better modified before it has to be used in anger. If one really wants the pendants to run down inside the boom, then each should emerge through an exit plate in the side of the boom just forward of each cheek block, which can be fitted in the normal way. Personally, I would rather see the pendants run down the outside of the boom, where they can be carefully watched for chafe, and easily replaced. I cannot believe that they can cause any noticeable windage, even on a racing boat.

With any of these slab reefing systems it must be appreciated that there is an enormous stress placed on the reefing pendant, particularly when going to windward. Because of the high loads, the pendant can be very susceptible to chafe, especially where it passes through the leech cringle. It is essential that any such cringle is smooth and well rounded, so that it cannot cut through the rope. The rope selected for the pendant should be quite thick, about the same size as the sheets used on the boat. All too often we have seen skinny little reefing pendants used, that are likely to break as soon as the going gets tough.

A few years ago, we were sailing in the Virgin Islands with some friends on a sixty-foot cutter. We had a reef tied down in the mainsail for the heavy winter Trade winds that were blowing, and we were hammering along to windward. Without any warning the reefing pendant snapped, and in an instant the sail ripped right across along the line of the reef points. It was just as if a giant zipper had been undone. The sail was just about totally destroyed before we could get it down. So, it is very important to keep a close eye on the state of the pendants. Braided rope, of the kind often used for sheets, will stand chafe a little better than ordinary three-strand laid rope. The smoother surface of the braided rope will also let it run more smoothly through the cringles. A good dodge to increase the life of the pendant is to make it a few feet too long. After each serious use, it can be shortened by an inch or two where it is attached to the boom. This makes sure that a new piece of rope bears on the cringle each time.

*   *   *

For an existing boat already fitted with a slab-reefing system, there are relatively easy ways to modify it to make reefing possible without venturing on deck, and without spending a fortune. When a sail is slab reefed, and the points are tied in, the whole sail depends upon the reefing pendant. If that breaks the sail is likely to be torn, perhaps beyond repair. One safety precaution is to tie another line through the leech cringle and round the boom, to give a second line of defence should the pendant part. This does, however, mean working on deck, reaching for the end of the boom, which is exactly what we are trying to avoid. It is definitely worth doing, though, if one is still at anchor and tying in a reef before a long passage that is expected to be rough.

If the rig is fitted with lazy jacks, it is often possible to sail with the reef in, but without tying in the points. If the pendant should break then, it is much less likely that the sail will be torn. The only time we have ever had a problem when

sailing with a sail that was slab reefed without the points
tied in was when we were caught in a tropical rain squall. It
rained so hard that the reefed part of the sail started to fill up
with water, and in next to no time we had a bag with about
fifty gallons of water in it hanging under the boom. It is con-
ceivable that the same thing could happen to a small boat
caught in breaking seas. However, even if you do decide that
it is more prudent to tie in the reef points, the job will be
much easier if lazy jacks are fitted, because at least the sail
will not be flogging all over the place while you are trying to
tie them in. So, for my money, lazy jacks are an essential
part of any slab-reefing system.

Roller Reefing

When reefing a mainsail by rolling it up along one edge, it is
possible to roll up either the foot or the luff of the sail. Let's
look at each way in turn, and see what advantages and disadvantages there are to each type of system.

If we are going to roll up one edge of the sail, it seems to
me that the obvious one to roll up is the foot, since it is so
much shorter than the luff. We will look first at the systems
that involve rolling up the foot of the sail.

Reefing the Sail Along the Foot

Rolling the sail around the boom is not a new idea. Such
systems have come in and out of fashion over the years. Not
too long ago everybody who was anybody had roller reefing
mainsails. The first 'proper' boat that I owned was a big old
gaff cutter, which was built around the turn of the century.
She had a monstrous great mechanism at the forward end of
the boom, which consisted of a worm-drive gear that rotated
the boom. In our case, the machinery was operated by
cranking a great big handle that went into the side of the
thing. This meant standing next to the mast while trying to
reef or unreef. However, it would not be too difficult to

arrange some way of working the mechanism from the cockpit. This could be done with a mechanical linkage, a hydraulic drive, or by using an electric motor.

The biggest problem that we had was that it put in a lousy reef. As the sail started to be wrapped around the boom, the luff rope tended to build up all in one place, while the leech of the sail effectively moved along the boom with each turn. The net result was that the outer end of the boom dropped down towards the water as more sail was reefed in.

We were able to combat this somewhat by throwing in a sailbag and an old sweater or two. These got wrapped into the sail near the leech, making the boom effectively thicker in that area. This caused more of the leech to get wound in with each turn, and kept the boom more or less horizontal.

The proper way would have been to fasten three or four long tapered wooden wedges along the boom, with their thicker ends aft. Such wedges are called whelps, and they effectively increase the diameter of the boom towards the outer end. Again, this increase in diameter causes more sail to be wound up at the leech, and stops the boom from drooping as the sail is wound in.

13. Boom fitted with whelps.

For roller reefing to work even half-way well, the sail must be cut with roller reefing in mind. The first prerequisite is that when the sail is set, the boom and mast must be at right angles to each other. If the angle between the boom and mast is anything other than ninety degrees, it will be imposs-

29

ible to roll the sail neatly round the boom. The shape of the leech of the sail is also crucial. A sail with a big roach and long battens is not likely to roll round the boom too neatly. Even if the sail is made so that the battens are parallel to the foot, by the time the sail is rolled round the boom a few times, it is most unlikely that the battens will roll neatly into the bundle. They will probably have to be removed in turn, as they reach the boom. This is an extra chore that involves being up on deck, reaching up for the leech of the sail. If roller reefing round the boom is the chosen option, it is better to have a sail that is designed to set without battens. This will mean that the leech is cut straight, or more probably slightly hollowed.

When the sail is being reefed down, the luff has to come free of the mast as the sail is rolled onto the boom. This means that if the sail is attached to the mast with slides, they must be released in turn from the track to allow the luff of the sail to roll up onto the boom. A sail that uses a boltrope which fits into an extrusion is probably better for this method of reefing. The boltrope is more likely to lie flat if there are no slides that have to get wrapped into the sail. Also when the time comes to shake out the reef, with a system using slides, somebody will have to be up there at the mast threading all those slides back onto the track. With a boltrope and extrusion, if the lead is correctly arranged, and there is perhaps a roller-type feeding mechanism mounted on the mast just below the luff groove, the sail should feed itself off the boom back into the groove.

Once the sail has been reefed, by wrapping it round the boom, it is no longer possible to attach a kicking strap in the normal way. The boom fittings are covered by the wrapped up sail. The windier conditions that require the sail to be reefed are just those that most require the use of a kicking strap for the sail to set effectively. The usual answer is to use a reefing claw. This is a device that fits around the boom and

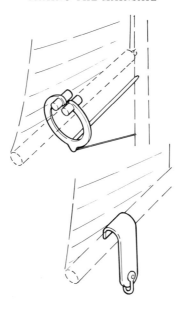

14. Claw ring and reefing claw.

the sail bundle, and allows the kicking strap to be attached to it.

The claw can be either in the form of a hook that clips over the boom, or a ring that partially encloses the boom.

The advantage of the claw ring is that the boom can be rotated in either direction when reefing, and it is usually better to rotate the boom so that the sail is on the leeward side of the boom when reefing. This presupposes that the reefing mechanism is happy to work in either direction. Those that incorporate a non-reversible ratchet will operate in only one direction. It is desirable for such a claw-ring to have good-sized rollers, to minimise chafe of the sail. If a hook is used it should be well padded for the same reason.

Whether a ring or a hook is used, it must be held in its correct place along the boom, otherwise the force of the kicking strap will pull it along the boom towards the mast. The best way to hold the claw in place is to use a compression tube, mounted beneath the boom, running between it and the mast. An alternative is to use a line running from the outer boom-end fitting to the claw. This line will stop the claw from being pulled towards the mast, but it may well show a tendency to get wound into the sail when the boom is being rotated.

Another alternative that we have used on occasion, when a proper claw ring was not available, is to rig a line beneath the boom, running between the end swivel and the gooseneck. The kicking strap is attached to the line, part way along, and will work quite well. The line will put considerable compressive loads on the boom, and the end swivel must be able to withstand the strong sideways pull, but it is a viable way to rig the kicking strap.

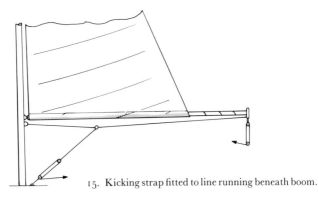

15. Kicking strap fitted to line running beneath boom.

There is at least one commercially available mechanism that winds the sail up inside the boom. This would enable the kicking strap to remain in place on the outside of the boom, but otherwise I can see no real benefit of such a system. The boom itself should be well able to withstand the torsional forces involved in winding up the sail, so any system that involves a separate torsional member inside the boom has got to be heavier, and more expensive, than a system that uses the boom itself.

With any roller-reefing system, we are relying on the reefing mechanism to stop the boom from suddenly turning and releasing the reefed portion of the sail. If the reefing mechanism fails, we may suddenly find ourselves with too much sail, and short of dropping the whole lot, no way to reduce the sail area. A worthwhile safety precaution is to have a row, or perhaps even two rows of eyelets, and the appropriate luff and leech cringles sewn into the sail, to enable a reef to be tied into the sail should the reefing mechanism fail. It would also perhaps be prudent to use such eyelets and cringles to back up the roller-reefing mechanism whenever conditions allowed.

The actual reefing mechanism should be chosen with care. The second offshore boat that I owned was a thirty-two-foot Bermudan sloop. She had a roller-reefing system that relied on a simple ratchet to stop the boom from being unrolled by the reefed sail. Taking in a reef was simple enough, a lever with a second ratchet rotated the boom quite easily. The problem came when it was time to unreef. It was very difficult to unreef a bit at a time, the ratchet had a tendency to release the boom completely, and all the sail would unwind in an instant. This mechanism, together with wire halyards on reel winches, made reefing and unreefing on this boat really quite a dangerous operation.

We have seen a more modern equivalent of this type of reefing mechanism, that has a crank handle which passes through the mast and rotates the boom through a universal joint in the gooseneck. The boom is stopped from rotating either by a ratchet, or by locking the handle in position. This sytem is adequate for small sails, where it has the advantage of the direct action rotating the boom quickly. For any sail over about two hundred square feet, an inordinately long handle would be required to control the boom with ease and safety. There is the danger that the boom, and hence the handle, might start flying round out of control if the ratchet failed to grip, or when the handle was released for unreefing.

The better solutions use a worm drive to turn the boom. There is little danger that the pressure of the sail will be able to rotate the boom against the worm. This does mean that the reefing gear must be physically turned to let sail out when unreefing rather than simply releasing it, but this way it can be done in a controlled manner, without the sail taking charge. Also with a worm-gear system there is less chance of the boom being released accidentally and the sail suddenly unwinding itself.

The late Angus Primrose spent a lot of time experimenting with roller-reefing systems and devising ways to control them from the cockpit. The system he finally used for his mainsail employed a continuous loop of rope, which ran over serrated sheaves. One of these was attached to the boom near the gooseneck, and one was mounted in the cockpit. When the cockpit one was turned with a winch handle, it made the rope rotate the other one, which in turn made the boom go round to roll up the sail. The device certainly worked, and would not be too expensive to duplicate. However, the sail would have to feed in and out of the mast track perfectly if one were to avoid going on deck at all. I would also suspect that a very deep reef, with lots of rolls of sail around the boom, might require a helping hand to pull the leech out along the boom if the sail is to set well. Also, like so many roller-reefing systems, the integrity of the reef depends entirely on a single piece of line. If that snaps, then you get full sail, ready or not. Certainly though, this would be a system to think about for improving an existing roller-reefing arrangement.

The alternative to rolling the sail up along the foot is to

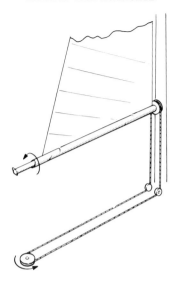

16. Continuous line rotating boom from cockpit.

roll it up along the luff. Let's now look at what is involved with such a system.

Reefing the Sail Along the Luff

The earliest luff-reefing systems used a sail with a wire luff. The sail was hoisted close behind the mast, and there were swivels just above and below the sail to allow the luff to rotate. The rotating was done by having the sail tacked down to a drum which had a rope wrapped around it. By pulling on the rope the drum turned, and the sail was wound round the luff wire.

It was soon found that the wire could not withstand the twisting forces involved when the sail was set partially reefed. The wire luff was soon replaced by a solid extrusion, which was still suspended a few inches abaft the mast. This more rigid extrusion allowed the sail to be set reefed, but it was still necessary to set the luff up very tight, otherwise it sagged away, spoiling the set of the sail. This type of system had two major shortcomings. The extra tension added considerably to the compressive load on the mast, and because the mainsail was no longer attached to the mast, the sail could not help to support it. Such a mast often 'pumps' when going to windward.

To withstand the extra compression the section of the mast has to be increased, and to reduce the 'pumping' effect, extra rigging, such as an inner forestay needs to be fitted to support the upper section of the mast. Both of these remedies add to the weight and cost of the rig.

The development of this type of reefing arrangement more or less stagnated until Ted Hood introduced his 'Stowaway' system. This uses a special mast section that has in effect an enormous luff groove. Inside this part of the mast there is a rotatable extrusion to which the luff of the sail is attached. To reef, or indeed to furl the sail, the luff extrusion is rotated, and the sail is wound up inside the mast.

17. Section through a stowaway mast, with sail partially wound around luff extrusion.

When the sail is set, either completely, or partially reefed, any load on the sail pulls the extrusion against the inside face of the slot. This means that the mast can support the luff of the sail, so the extrusion does not have to be set up very tight to keep the luff straight. This reduces the compressive loading on the mast, and the sail can also now help to support the mast. The pull of the sail along the after edge of the mast will help to reduce any pumping in a seaway, without resorting to extra rigging.

There are several ways that can be used to rotate the luff extrusion. It can be done with a simple drum and rope at the bottom. This is the cheapest and simplest way, and it is easy to lead the line back to the cockpit for in-cockpit reefing. The only real drawback to such a simple system is one of reliability. If that reefing line were to chafe through and part, you might suddenly be presented with full sail just when you least needed it.

A mechanical worm-drive mechanism is less likely to fail in this way, but it does cost a little more, and might prove more complicated to control from the cockpit. On bigger boats, a frequent alternative is an electric motor mounted in the base of the mast, driving a worm gear. Such a device can give push-button reefing and furling, at least until the salt water finds its way into the electrics. The answer here is to install a good manual back-up system.

With any reefing system of this type, the sail is set loose footed on the boom. The clew of the sail is held by an outhaul, which runs through a slide which is mounted on a track on top of the boom. This system holds the clew of the sail down towards the boom whether the whole sail is set or it is reefed.

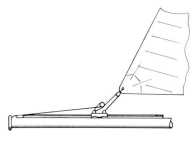

18. Outhaul and slide on loose-footed luff-reefing mainsail.

When the sail is reefed, the outhaul moves forward a considerable distance along the boom, possibly as far as halfway along. Since the sail is loose footed, all the load is taken by the clew, rather than being spread out along the foot of the sail. This can lead to problems with the boom bending, particularly if it is sheeted at the end, so this type of reefing will often call for a larger section of boom.

Since the entire sail gets rolled up inside the mast when it is furled, it cannot of course have any battens. Provided that the sail is cut with this in mind, with a hollow leech, that should not present any real problems. The small amount of sail area lost should not worry most cruising boats.

Theoretically, you should be able to put any number of reefs in such a system. However, when you remember that the entire length of the luff extrusion is being rotated just by twisting it at the bottom, you can perhaps realise that it is not a good idea to set the sail with a very small reef in. Most manufacturers suggest that for the first reef you wind in half of the area of the sail, to reduce the twisting stress on the extrusion. If the sail is set with just a roll or two round the extrusion, the twisting forces can be great enough to shear off the strongest extrusion. It is worth heeding the manufacturers' suggestions with regard to this, and it is a good idea to mark the foot of the sail where the first reef should be. This saves any guesswork. With a triangular sail, the area is approximately halved when one third of the foot is rolled in.

There are several drawbacks to this type of system, not the least of which is cost. It would be very expensive to convert an existing rig, as probably neither the mast nor the mainsail, and possibly not even the boom off the old rig would be any use on the new rig. Even on a new boat, the system is very expensive, involving special mast sections and the extrusion, etc.

There is also an unexpected drawback to this type of rig in that it is very noisy. The wind blowing across the large slot in the mast sets up a howling that has to be heard to be believed. It is possible to hoist a canvas strip up the mast groove when moored to stop the noise but unfortunately for their neighbours, not too many people seem to bother.

Another seemingly obvious way to reef the luff of the sail is to wrap it round the mast. It is entirely possible to rotate an unstayed mast and to roll the sail up from the luff. Several people have experimented with this idea, with mixed success. 'Blondie' Hasler spent several years working with just such a rig, but he eventually abandoned it as impractical. The most serious problem he found was that when the sail was reefed, the wind kept getting into the rolled-up part of the sail and started shaking it loose and making it flap about high up on the mast.

Conclusions

Any roller-reefing system offers the theoretical attraction of an infinite number of reefs, but as we have seen, the mechanical limitations often dictate that the first reef be a big one. This is more likely to be a problem on the luff-reefing systems than on those that reef the foot. Provided that the reefing mechanism itself is strong enough, the boom should be capable of withstanding the stress of sailing with just a roll or two of sail reefed down. Doing the same thing with a long luff extrusion could lead to problems.

Roller-reefing systems do not fail safe. If anything breaks, one is likely to end up with full sail, perhaps just when you least need it. On a system that rolls up the foot, it is easy to fit a back-up points-reefing system, so that if the roller reefing should fail, a slab reef can still be tied in. On most of the luff-rolling systems the sail can be lowered only if it is completely unfurled. If the mechanism jammed with a roll or two of the sail reefed, it would be quite difficult to get the sail down in bad conditions. Having said that, to be fair, there are surprisingly few failures of this type of equipment.

Either luff- or foot-rolling methods can be set up to be operated from the cockpit, yet they are rarely seen to be so. It may be a little complicated to get such a system working from the cockpit, and it is likely to be quite expensive, but it is possible.

All roller-reefing systems have an inherent area of high stress: the point at which the boom or luff extrusion is rotated. We have the technology and the materials to build everything strong enough, but I can't help feeling that a system which spreads the load more evenly through the rig is less likely to fail in the long term. Slab reefing does eliminate this one area of high stress, but when we come to look at some other rigs we will see that some of them, particularly the Chinese junk rig, have no areas of high stress.

My own choice for reefing the mainsail on a Bermudan-rigged boat would be to go for a good slab-reefing system, to be used with a set of lazy jacks. Leading all the controls to the cockpit is easy, and the system is basically very reliable. If the pendants run outside the boom, all parts of the system are visible, and so can easily be inspected. Maintenance is minimal and repairs are easy. If the system is set up carefully, I feel that it is in fact easier and quicker to use than roller reefing, and usually the sail sets better. With the lazy jacks fitted, even furling the sail is no problem. Finally, the best slab-reefing system is cheaper than even the most basic roller-reefing system.

As we come to some of the alternative rigs, we will see that several of them offer even easier reefing and sail control than any of these systems, and my own choice is to move away from the Bermudan rig completely. We have seen how the reefing system on an existing Bermudan-rigged boat can perhaps be improved, but for those people considering a new boat, or a complete re-rig, then I would suggest a close look at some of the other available rigs. Most of these alternative rigs have the added advantage that they manage quite nicely without a headsail, which certainly helps to make life easier. Before we move on to these other rigs though, for those people who have a Bermudan-rigged boat, let's look at ways to make life with a headsail more tolerable.

3

Headsails—To Change, Reef, or Furl?

The racing brigade would feel lost if they did not have at least half a dozen headsails to choose from. Every keen racer must have a streak of masochism in his make-up! Why else would he spend so much time up there on the pitching foredeck, breaking fingernails in the middle of the night, fighting a flogging jib in the pouring rain?

For the cruising fraternity, there are several good reasons for doing things differently. Apart from the sheer unpleasantness of changing headsails in poor conditions, all those headsails have to be bought in the first place. Once they each in turn are all nice and wet, they have to be dragged down below and stowed somewhere. Not only do they get everything else wet and salty, but bundled up sails take an enormous amount of room.

Last, but by no means least, struggling out there on the foredeck, particularly on a dark and dirty night, must be one of the most dangerous things that a yachtsman will ever do in his lifetime. There has to be a better way.

Changing Headsails
If we are determined to change headsails, let's at least give that some thought, and try to make the job as easy and safe as possible.

The most difficult type of headsail to change is one that does not remain hanked onto the forestay when it is lowered. The racing boats almost all use streamlined foils which either replace, or fit over the forestay. The luff of the headsail has a miniature boltrope which slides up inside a groove in the foil. When the sail is dropped, the boltrope slides down out of the groove, and the sail is now only positively attached to the boat by the tack. The rest of the sail is free to be blown about by the wind.

The racers get around this problem by having an army of crew ready to grab the sail as it comes off the foil. For short-handed cruising, such an arrangement is positively dangerous. It is so much safer to use a sail that is hanked onto the forestay, because when such a sail is lowered the whole length of the luff remains attached to the forestay, which makes it easier for the rest of the sail to be brought under control.

We have found that it is much easier to hank on a new headsail if the hanks are threaded onto a short length of line in the correct order. Then each can be transferred in turn to the forestay, with less chance that they will be put on in the wrong order. With this arrangement, the luff of the sail is held under control as soon as the sail is tacked down. Those hanks that are not yet on the forestay are held in place by the piece of line. When I had a sloop that boasted a choice of three headsails, I spliced a short length of line onto the tack of each sail to take the hanks. So long as the hanks were always replaced on the line each time that the sail was lowered, it always came out of the bag with the hanks in the right order.

There have been several commercial systems offered from time to time that do essentially the same thing. Various cartridges and slides have been devised that collect the hanks together, and either hold them, or feed them onto the forestay. Unfortunately racing is where the money is, and since hardly any serious racing boats still use hanked sails, development of this type of device has ground to a halt.

One of the worst aspects of changing headsails is having to drag the wet sails down below. Not only is this in itself dangerous, involving either an open forehatch, or sail bags being dragged along the deck, but all that salt water being brought down below soon makes the whole boat damp.

Lana and I once delivered a forty-eight-foot ketch across the Atlantic, and she had some big sausage-shaped sail bags which were more or less permanently attached to the toe-rail on either bow. When changing headsails, the old sail was just dropped into its bag, the zipper done up, and there the sail lived until it was needed again. This saved dragging the wet sail across the deep-pile, pale-beige fitted carpet down below. However, whether the sails would have remained there safely it we had had to face any serious weather fortunately remained a hypothetical question.

A rather more seaworthy alternative, which achieved the same result was seen on a Polish OSTAR boat a few races ago. She had three forestays arranged in a triangle. The forwardmost one took any light-weather sails. The other two each went down into the forward ends of two long troughs that were built into the deck. The Number Two and Three jibs were respectively hanked onto each forestay, and they could lie in their trough, covered with a hatch, until needed. Changing between these two sails simply involved dropping one sail into its trough and shutting the lid, then opening the other and hoisting the new sail. The sheets remained attached all the time. Each trough was self-draining, and the whole thing looked seaworthy

*   *   *

Although it is possible to make headsail changing easier, an actual sail-change is going to require somebody up there on the foredeck. This is one of sailing's more dangerous aspects, so let's concentrate on ways to change the area of the headsail from the safety of the cockpit.

Reefing Headsails

It would certainly be nice to have one headsail for all conditions. Roller-reefing headsails are often touted as just that, but are they in practice? What are their limitations and what are the alternatives?

The theory of the roller-reefing headsail is delightfully simple, although the better systems show a considerable subtlety of design. The basic idea is that the sail is rolled up round its luff until it is the size that is required for the present conditions.

The idea has been with us for many years. The first recorded use of a roller-furling jib was by Captain E. du Boulay towards the end of the last century. He used a wooden luff spar which fitted over the wire forestay, rather like many of the systems that we see in use today. He did not have the benefits of the high strength light alloys that we have now, and the reliability of his system was limited by the strength of the long thin wooden luff spars that he was forced to use.

The Wykeham-Martin roller-furling gear appeared on the ends of numerous bowsprits around the turn of the century. The gear was a very basic rotating drum which fitted between the end of the bowsprit and the tack of the jib. The head of the sail was fitted with a swivel so that the jib could be rolled round the luff without twisting the halyard.

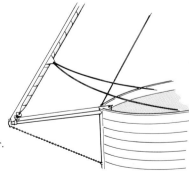

19. Wykeham-Martin jib furler.

A rope is wound around the drum, and by pulling on the rope, the drum is rotated and the jib is wound round the luff wire. With such a system the jib could be quickly and easily furled without anybody venturing out onto the end of the bowsprit. On the gaff cutters that were so common in those days, a furled jib and a deep reef in the main would leave a very snug rig of staysail and reefed main. On the bigger boats there was often provision for tying a slab reef in the staysail to further reduce the sail area.

With this type of roller-furling headsail there was no chance of setting the sail partially reefed. It was an all-or-nothing type of system. The wire luff in the jib could not stand being twisted at the bottom, while effectively being untwisted higher up by the load of the sheet on the sail. Such an arrangement is considered to be roller furling rather than roller reefing, so beware of systems advertised as roller furling, if what you want is roller reefing.

To try to get around the problem of the luff wire twisting, some sails were made with a chain luff. When the chain was set up tight it could stand considerable twisting forces, but the play between the links allows the top to lag half a turn or more behind if the bottom is being twisted to roll the sail up. Again, a chain luff was found to be better suited to roller furling than reefing, except in the rare case where a specially designed chain was used.

To achieve roller reefing, the jib must be set up on a more rigid extrusion that can withstand these twisting forces. These extrusions are of two basic types. One type is of a hollow section, usually made of an aluminium alloy, which fits over a normal wire forestay, and rotates round the forestay on a series of bearings. The second type actually replaces the forestay, and is a solid rod, usually stainless steel, which is extruded with an integral groove to take the luff of the sail.

It would appear that there are several advantages in using

46

20. Section through hollow alloy extrusion fitted over forestay (left), and through solid rod extrusion (right).

a system which uses hollow extrusions which fit over the forestay. If such an extrusion is damaged, there is a good chance that the forestay itself will remain intact, and little likelihood that the mast will fall down.

This type of system is usually composed of a series of interlocking extrusions, each some six to ten feet long. If the extrusion is damaged, it is usually possible to take the forestay down, dismantle the extrusions and replace just the damaged section. If a new piece of extrusion is not immediately available, then it might be possible to rearrange the sections so that the damaged piece is at the top, where the stresses are the least.

It is very impotant that the sections lock together strongly at the joints, because should one of these joints come undone, the sail will be pinched in the luff groove and it will be impossible to lower the sail. It is also important that the joints are a very good fit, as if there is any play at all, they will work loose, and perhaps become separated. At the charter company where we have been working for the past few years, when they assemble new extrusions, they bed the joints together in silicone rubber. They have found that it will act as enough of an adhesive to reduce the chance of movement, but will not stick the parts together so well that they can never be taken apart. Since they have been doing this they have found the life of the extrusions to be considerably extended. The silicone rubber will also help to keep water out of the joints, and reduce the risk of corrosion.

With a solid extrusion there is no choice. If the extrusion is damaged, the whole thing must be replaced. A common way for these extrusions to be damaged is to allow a spinnaker pole to hit the forestay, so if you have a roller-reefing headstay, and feel compelled to fly a spinnaker, then do so with caution.

If a solid extrusion should shear off under the enormous twisting loads that it must endure when the sail is set reefed, then there is no forestay, and the whole rig could well be in jeopardy.

Whichever type is selected, solid or hollow, try to get one that is basically circular in section. The current trend is towards pear-shaped streamlined sections, which look very racy, but they are much harder to turn than a round section, as they roll the sail in with a jerky motion.

Whether a hollow or solid extrusion is used, it must be strong, it has to withstand tremendous twisting forces. All the roller-reefing systems presently available use some kind of mechanism at the bottom of the extrusion to rotate it along the whole length. As the sail starts to roll up during reefing, the foot of the sail moves up the forestay. When the sail is substantially reefed the pull of the foot of the sail, which is effectively trying to unroll the sail, is several feet up the forestay. The extrusion is being held against rotation by the drum or other mechanism at the bottom, so the extrusion must be able to withstand these two opposing forces.

To avoid unfair loading on the extrusion, most manufacturers recommend that when the sail is reefed, the first reef should be substantial. They usually suggest reefing about half the area of the sail for the first reef. As we mentioned when talking about the roller-reefing mainsails, to reef half the area of the sail we have to roll up about one third of the foot. Again, it is a good idea to mark on the foot of the sail

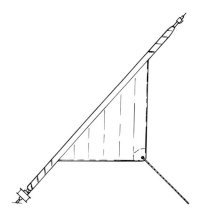

21. Reefed headsail—showing foot of sail part way up the forestay.

where this first reef is, then there is less chance of putting in too small a reef and perhaps twisting the extrusion.

To put in a small reef with just one or two rolls around the extrusion, and then to crank the sheet in hard, will perhaps put such a load on the extrusion that it will twist, corkscrew fashion. This will usually result in the luff of the sail becoming trapped in the groove of the extrusion so that it can no longer be lowered. If the extrusion is very badly twisted, then the only way to get the sail down is to take down the complete forestay, or to cut the sail free from the luff tape, leaving the tape in the groove, and lowering the sail. There are surprisingly few of this type of failure, and most of the ones that we have seen have usually been caused by abuse or carelessness.

A more common failure is in the mechanism for rotating the extrusion, and some of these failures can be quite spectacular.

The majority of the systems rely on a simple drum, mounted at the base of the extrusion, that has a rope wrapped round it to control the rotation. As the sail is unrolled by pulling on the sheet, the extrusion rotates the drum, which winds up the rope, or perhaps wire, onto the drum. To roll up the sail, just pull on the furling line. As it unwinds off the drum, it rotates the drum, which in turn rotates the extrusion and so winds up the sail. What could be easier?

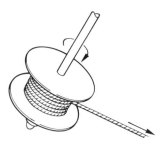

22. Drum and furling line.

The most common weakness in the system is the furling line itself. In most cases the diameter of the drum is only about twice the diameter of the rolled up sail bundle when the sail is half reefed, which means that the load on the furling line is about half of the total load on the jib sheet, that is doing its best to unroll the sail. We are all aware that the jib sheets withstand considerable loads, yet all too often one sees a very thin furling line secured to a rather small cleat, which is perhaps just screwed to the cockpit coaming.

The failure of the furling line, or indeed of the cleat to which it is secured when the jib is set reefed, can result in suddenly getting full sail, probably just when you least need it. We met one sixty-footer in the Bahamas whose furling line had snapped when they were sailing with a much reefed jib in about fifty knots of winds.

When the line parted, the jib unrolled instantaneously to its full size. It unrolled with such a bang that the clew of the sail tore off at once, leaving the whole sail flogging in the wind. Before the crew could lower the sail, the violent flogging tore the forestay off the stemhead fitting. The sail, furling gear, and forestay were now all streaming from the masthead. I feel that the crew were lucky to save the rig, indeed to save the boat. All because of a furling line that parted.

There is ample scope for development of a better mechanism for rotating the luff extrusion. Several companies offer an electric drive. The motor is mounted on the stemhead, and rotates the extrusion through a worm gear. This theoretically will give push-button reefing or furling. With the worm drive there is little chance of the sail suddenly unfurling itself, but having the motor mounted in such an exposed position, there is a strong possibility, I would think, of getting water into the works. The units that we have seen have provision for putting in a standard winch handle to operate the worm gear manually, should the motor fail.

It would be possible to use a similar worm gear, but to plan on turning the worm manually, perhaps using an endless line that runs back to the cockpit. Pulling the line one way would unroll the sail, and pulling it the other way would roll it up, and at no time would there be a risk of the sail taking charge.

23. Worm drive rotating extrusion using endless line.

With the commonly used rope and drum system there is a very real danger that the sail will take charge, particularly when the sail is let out on a breezy day. It is very important to let the sail out slowly. If it is allowed to rush out unchecked, it could put an unfair shock load on the system; also the furling line is likely to become hopelessly bunched and tangled around the rapidly spinning drum. The line must be let out steadily and tension maintained all the time. With a reasonably sized sail on a breezy day the pull on the furling line can be considerable, so play safe, and keep a turn around the cleat as you pay out the line, and avoid at best a nasty rope burn.

Likewise with this type of system, when trying to reef or furl the sail on a breezy day, the pull on the line may prove too much for a family crew to manage, without resorting to a winch. If you do use a winch for the furling line, make very sure that the gear is free to turn. With the power of a winch it is all too easy to turn a minor tangle into a major breakage.

A properly designed worm gear could give sufficient mechanical advantage to allow for turning by hand, without using a winch. This would minimise the risk of doing damage should something unseen be fouled.

It would be nice to see a furling gear, regardless of how it was rotated, that had a grease nipple fitted. It is not so much that the mechanism really needs much lubrication, but if it was packed with grease to the point where one could see it oozing out, then there would be little chance of any water finding its way in. When seawater does get in and evaporates, salt crystals get left behind. This build-up of salt will make the gear gradually stiffen up, and will certainly accelerate the wear of the bearings.

As the sail is rolled up round the luff, the clew will tend to move forward. It will rise somewhat as well, but basically it will move forward. For the reefed sail to set properly, the lead for the sheet will also have to move forward. If it is not

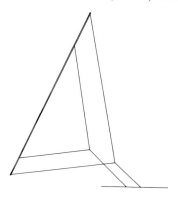

24. Showing positions for the sheet fairlead with full sail
and with the sail reefed.

moved, it will be impossible to tighten the leech of the sail to
go to windward. The reefed sail is probably already fuller
than one might wish, and if the leech is left slack, then the
windward performance will really suffer.

On many boats the jib sheet fairleads are mounted on a
track. In theory, as the jib is reefed in, the fairlead is simply
moved forward on the track. Easier written than done. Few
fairleads can be moved while there is a heavy load on the
sheet, and if the sheet is cast off and the sail allowed to flog, it
is still difficult, and often very dangerous to try to move the
fairlead with the sheet flapping wildly about.

A much safer way is to move the fairlead on the windward
side to the new position, then tack over. The other fairlead
can now be moved, and the boat tacked back again. This is
only possible if one has a good idea of where the new sheeting position will be, so it is well worth marking the track for
the position of the fairleads when the sail is reefed. This
could be done at the same time as when the foot of the sail is
being marked for the first reef, as it is certainly much easier
to experiment with sheeting positions on a nice calm day,

rather than when reefing in anger on a dark and dirty night.

Moving the fairleads in this way means that somebody has to go on deck twice, and we are trying to eliminate that sort of thing. Also two 'unnecessary' extra tacks might prove to be the last straw for a tired crew, so what other ways are there?

It is feasible to have two sets of fairleads on the track, one in the full sail position, and one in the reefed position. Once the sail is reefed, a spare jib sheet can be led through the new fairlead and tied on to the clew of the sail. The old sheet is cast off, and the load taken on the new sheet. In this way the lead can be changed without the sail flogging too much, without anybody going near it while it is flogging, and without having to do the two extra tacks. It does still require a fair amount of deck work, and somebody has to reach out to the clew of the sail.

If a small tackle is rigged onto each fairlead, then it is possible to move the fairleads from the safety of the cockpit. Normally only a tackle is needed to move the fairlead forward. The upward pull of the sheet is usually sufficient to move it aft.

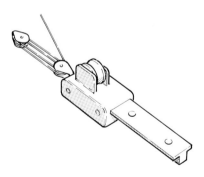

25. Movable sheet fairlead and tackle.

It is a good plan to fit a stop on the track behind the fairlead in the normal full sail position. The tackle can be left slack, with the fairlead held in place by the stop when sailing with full sail.

When the sail is being reefed, before the sheet is hardened in, the tackle is tightened, and the fairlead moved forward. It is helpful to mark the line for the tackle in the appropriate place, so that the fairlead can be positioned in the right spot. With this simple system, nobody has to leave the cockpit, nobody has to risk getting whipped by the sheet, yet the fairlead is adjusted to let the sail be sheeted to the best advantage.

Reefing a sail by rolling it up along the luff will cause the Centre of Effort of the sail to move forward. If both the mainsail and the jib are reefed in this way, it is possible that the balance of the boat could be upset.

The basic idea of these roller-reefing systems is deceptively simple. As we have seen, the luff of the sail is wound around the rotating extrusion somewhat like a window blind. The subtlety creeps in when we try to get the reefed sail to set well. It is not just the position of the sheet that affects the set of the sail. As the sail is rolled up there is a tendency for the foot and the leech to roll up tighter than the 'belly' or the bunt of the sail. This results in the sail becoming progressively fuller as it is being reefed, just when you want it to be getting flatter. There are a couple of different ways that can be used to try to get the sail to keep its shape when reefed.

26. Roller reefing gear with swivel on the drum for the tack, and for the head at the halyard.

Some manufacturers incorporate an extra swivel at the tack and at the head of the sail.

With such a solution when the drum and the extrusion begin to rotate, the tack and head of the sail which are not attached directly to the extrusion or drum tend to lag behind. For about the first complete turn, only the bunt of the sail is wound round the extrusion. This helps to flatten the sail, at least for the first reef. After that, though, the swivels have no further effect on flattening the sail as it is reefed more. The sail does set better, however, on a system of this type than if the whole sail is just wound bodily round the extrusion.

Another way to take some of the fullness out of the sail is to increase the effective diameter of the centre portion of the luff extrusion, so that more sail is wound up in the centre than at the ends. In theory, we could fit wooden whelps as we suggested on the boom, but it is easier to increase the thickness of the luff tabling in the central portions of the sail. As the sail is wound in, these thicker portions of the tabling will wind up more sail, and so flatten it somewhat. We have seen some people use layers of sticky tape up the luff to thicken it, but obviously it is better to have the thickened tabling permanently sewn onto the sail. Some sailmakers will use a tapered false boltrope sewn into the luff, with its thickest portion at the middle of the luff, which will have the same effect.

It is well worth shopping round for a sailmaker who is willing to cooperate in building a sail designed for roller reefing. Another detail worth specifying is tape loops at the head and tack, rather than the more commonly seen cringles. The cringles will tend to stand proud when the jib is rolled up, effectively increasing the diameter just where we want to reduce it to a minimum, whereas the tape loops will lie flat, and the sail can easily roll over them.

Since we know that the sail will have a tendency to get

progressively fuller as the sail is reefed, it is perhaps worth asking the sailmaker to cut the sail on the flat side initially. This way the sail is likely to set better over a wider range of conditions than one that is very full to begin with.

The sailmaker should also be aware of what type of roller-reefing gear you intend to use with the sail. With the type of hollow extrusions that go over a wire forestay, it is possible, even desirable to set the forestay up really tight, so there is little sag in the stay. With the systems that replace the forestay with a solid extrusion, they cannot be set up as tight, since the bearings that allow the extrusion to rotate take the entire load of the forestay. The sailmaker must estimate, and allow for the sag of the forestay to leeward, otherwise again, the sail is likely to be too full.

Some sailmakers are prepared to mix the weights of cloth used in the sail, using lighter weights near the luff, and heavier weights towards the leech. The lighter cloth near the luff will certainly help you to 'read' the sail when going to windward with full sail, and it may even help the shape of the sail. As the wind increases, and the sail is partially rolled

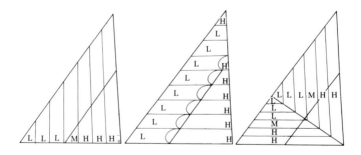

27. Examples of roller-furling jibs made with mixed weights of cloth, light, medium and heavy—showing how light areas are reefed away for strong winds.

up, it is the lighter cloth that is rolled up first, leaving just the heavier cloth to cope with the increasing wind. There are several ways that the cloth weights can be mixed, with no one way appearing vastly superior.

From what we have seen so far, we can appreciate that there are definite limitations to a roller-reefing headsail, and it is unlikely to be ideal for all conditions. What are the alternatives?

If we cannot expect the one sail to cope with all conditions, then perhaps we should limit the range over which we expect it to perform, and use other sails for conditions outside that range. One way we can do that is to take a leaf out of the old working sailors' book, and rig the boat as a cutter.

The cutter is a very good, flexible cruising rig. The jib can be set with roller-furling gear, and be designed to withstand going to windward in up to Force 5 or so. Above that, the jib can be furled, and the boat can continue with just the staysail and mainsail. The staysail could be set on roller-reefing gear, or have provision for tying in a slab reef. With a good cutter rig, the jib could be cut quite full, and of fairly light cloth, as it would never be set reefed, nor in very strong winds.

Another compromise that we have seen is to have two roller-reefing headsails set beside each other at the stemhead. One sail is made for light conditions, and the other for heavier going. Changing sails is just a question of rolling up one sail, and unrolling the other. This is a rather expensive solution, and in practice does require some deck work, since the sheets of the sail that is not being used have to be led forward to clear the sail that is in use.

A somewhat cheaper solution is to have a roller-reefing headsail that is designed to operate in winds of, say, Force 3 to 7. Then you have a separate wire forestay set up that can take a light-weight Number One genoa hanked on. In winds up to Force 3, the lightweight Number One is used. Before conditions get to the point where it is unpleasant or dangerous to be on the foredeck, the Number One is taken off and the roller-reefing headsail used. If one wanted to try and cover all eventualities, then as the Number One is taken off, a storm jib could be hanked on in its place, to be ready in case conditions really deteriorate.

Having a forestay in addition to the roller-reefing gear gives one a lot more flexibility, but there is a tendency for whichever forestay is not in use to foul the one that is, and perhaps cause chafe. In the days before roller-reefing headsails, it was quite common to have twin headstays. When both headstays were simply fastened down to the stemhead there were often problems. When a sail was set on one stay, that stay would sag somewhat with the load of the sail, and the lazy stay would tend to become quite slack, and flap about. A common way of solving, or at least limiting the slackness of the lazy stay, was to mount the two stays on either end of a pivoting bar, rather like a see-saw. This had the effect of equalising the strain on both stays, and keeping them equally tight.

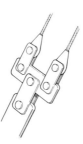

28. Twin headstays mounted on a pivoting bar at the stemhead.

If such a system were used with a roller-reefing system on one side, the pull of the sail and of the reefing line both in the same direction would put a tremendous twisting load on the fitting. It is possible to build a fitting that not only allows the two forestays to pivot on a bar so as to equalise the tensions, but also allows the whole thing to swivel so that the forestay in use is always abaft the lazy forestay.

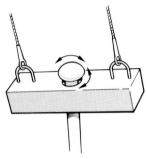

29. One way to make a stemhead fitting that allows the forestays to equalise tensions, and also to pivot, so that the forestay in use is abaft the other.

Until some enterprising manufacturer takes note, it would be better to mount the pivoting bar at or near the masthead, where the twisting forces will be much less than at the stemhead.

If the complications of a second forestay are too daunting, then it is possible to set other sails flying, that is, not hanked onto a stay. In Chapter 8 we will be looking at easy ways of handling light-weather sails, such as cruising spinnakers and drifters, which can be set flying in light conditions. For the storm jib, it is possible, but not easy also to set it flying.

If a storm jib is set flying it will need to be made with a heavy wire luff to withstand the extra strain, and it will have to be set up very tight indeed, using a winch or Highfield lever if it is not to sag hopelessly off to leeward. We only tried it once, on an old gaff cutter, but setting a storm jib flying is an interesting experience, as it not only flogs as the wind catches it, but it tends to oscillate wildly.

It is possible to rig an inner forestay just for the storm jib.

This can be set up using a Highfield lever, and the storm jib hanked on before conditions deteriorate too much. Under normal conditions the inner forestay is released and led down against the shrouds out of the way. Such a stay, when rigged, must be far enough away from the proper forestay not to cause any interference, nor would there then be any problem of one stay being tighter than the other. Such a system is often seen on some of the larger racing boats, and now it is beginning to appear on smaller cruising boats too. It is already fitted to at least one production cruising boat, the Rossiter Pintail.

Yet another alternative is to set the storm jib on its own special wire halyard. It can be hanked on to the fall of the halyard, which is led down to the deck and through a block where the storm jib is tacked down. The sail will not only be easier to hoist than if it is set flying, but it will also sag off to leeward much less; however, it will still not be as good as if it were set on a stay.

Whether the headsail is considered as roller-reefing or roller-furling, it is likely to be left up in the furled position for the whole season, even when the boat is not in use. It is indeed an enthusiastic owner who would take down the furled sail each time he gets back from sailing. Sunlight is the worst enemy of modern sailcloth, and even in temperate climes, if the sail is protected from the sun, its life will be considerably extended. An easy way to protect the furled sail is to sew onto the foot and leech of the sail a strip of protective material. The best material to use is an acrylic, as it stands up to sunlight well and is impervious to rot.

It is desirable to use a strip of acrylic as narrow as possible, but one that will still cover the sail when it is furled. Any more material than is absolutely necessary will add bulk to the leech and foot when the sail is being rolled up, and compound the problem of increasing fullness with reefing. The best way to see what width of cloth will suffice, is simply to measure between the rolls on the foot and leech when the sail is furled. The protective material will be wider on the leech than on the foot, assuming that the leech is longer than the foot of the sail.

Obviously the cover material must be on the outside of the roll of sail when it is furled. If the furling gear will only rotate in one direction to wind up the sail, care must be taken to ensure that the protective material is sewn on the correct side of the sail.

In theory, we could reef a headsail by setting it on a boom, and rolling it up along the foot. It would be much better to roll it round a short boom, than round a long luff extrusion. Unfortunately it is not practicable to have the foot of the sail at right angles to the forestay, so it is impossible to get the sail to wrap neatly around the boom.

Perhaps a system could be developed with a boom mounted part way up the forestay, at right angles to it, and when it was rotated, it would roll up the sail above and below it.

Conclusions

Roller-reefing headsails are perhaps not the cure-all that they have been touted to be, but if their limitations are realised, and they definitely do have some limitations, there is no doubt that they can make life much easier than just using conventional sails.

A roller-reefed sail often does not set too well, and when the sail is reefed, the Centre of Effort rises, which increases the heeling forces on the boat, which in turn reduces still further the amount of sail that the boat can carry.

Care should be taken to abide by the manufacturers' recommendations with regard to the safe first reef, otherwise it is quite easy to damage the gear. Some thought should be given about what to do should a failure occur. If the gear is damaged in such a way that the sail can neither be furled nor lowered, then one must consider other ways to douse the sail. On a small boat it might be possible to run off downwind to blanket the jib in the lee of the mainsail, and by grabbing the clew of the jib, roll the leech toward the luff. If the lower part of the sail is lashed to the forestay, the upper part could be frapped by wrapping the burgee halyard, or a spare headsail halyard round and round the bundle.

On a larger boat this would probably not be feasible, if only because the clew may well be too high to reach from the deck. In this case, if it has reached the point where the sail must come down, then consider sheeting the sail in hard, and cutting a little way up the luff tape close to the extrusion. Hopefully the tape will rip along the entire length and free it from the extrusion. It should then be possible to lower the sail without too much damage. Since the sail is now flying free from the forestay it may not be easy, but again if it is blanketed by the mainsail by virtue of running downwind, it should be possible to lower it.

If I was rigging a Bermudan-rigged boat for myself, the first thing that I would do is to step back a few years in time, and choose a rig with a big mainsail and small headsail, since generally the mainsail is the easier sail to handle. Probably the most acceptable compromise would be to have a roller-reefing jib designed for the middle range of conditions. With a light sail to play about with in nice weather, and a storm jib to be set up on a separate stay for heavy conditions, I would feel quite well prepared.

The racing boats tend to choose small mainsails and big headsails purely because they get a substantial benefit under the current rating rules. They give scant thought to ease of handling. Quite a lot of cruising catamarans, that can have few pretensions towards serious racing, also opt for a very small mainsail, and an enormous foretriangle. This does have the advantage of bringing the mast back, close to the cockpit, so the mainsail can be handled from inside the cockpit, but it leaves you with big headsails not only to raise, lower and reef or change, but also to winch in after every tack.

By contrast, the racing multihulls, usually unfettered by the rating rules of their single-hulled cousins, are tending to do just the reverse. They are now choosing big mainsails, often set on enormous streamlined wing masts, and very small headsails, or in some cases none at all. Perhaps this is one case when the cruisers can follow the racers and be on the right track.

For really serious offshore work, if for some reason I were locked into the Bermudan rig, I would perhaps choose a cutter, again with a big mainsail. The jib would be roller-furling, and the staysail set on a boom. With this rig, as conditions piped up, the jib could be furled, a deep reef put in the main, and you would have a nice snug self-tending rig for going to windward.

My actual choice, though, has been to get away from the headsail completely and its associated problems, and to choose a rig that manages quite nicely without. Some people are reluctant to lose the headsail, for fear that they will lose manoeuvrability. That might be so in the case of a boat with a single-masted rig, but, in our experience, that is not the case with a schooner- or ketch-rigged boat.

With our own boat, a thirty-five-foot junk-rigged schooner, we have found her to be more manoeuvrable under sail than most conventional boats. We cruised her quite extensively for three years without an engine, and delighted in sailing her into 'impossible' places. So let's look at the junk rig in detail, and see what other benefits it has, and face up to its shortcomings.

4

The Junk Rig

The junk rig has become almost synonymous with the concept of handling sails from in the cockpit. We will take a short look at the history of this rig, and see how it came to be adapted to Western use. Then we will look at its strengths and weaknesses, and try and decide how practical it really is for use on a cruising boat.

The History of the Junk Rig

The rig is more correctly called a Chinese Lugsail rig, but since the term junk rig has come into common usage, we will use it for brevity. The junk rig has a long and colourful history, in fact it is one of the oldest rigs still in use today. It has existed in China, substantially unchanged, for well over two thousand years. There are almost as many variations of it as there are Chinamen, but for our purposes we can define a junk sail as a balanced lugsail, with a vertical luff, and full length battens, with the sheet going to the ends of all or most of the battens.

When we call a sail balanced, that means that a portion of the sail, in the case of the junk somewhere between a sixth and a third of the area, extends forward of the mast. The Chinese found that there was little need for standing rigging to support the mast. They had no headsail requiring a tight forestay; the balanced sail and the sheet leading to each batten spread the load evenly, and in many cases it was found that the masts could support themselves, without complicated rigging.

The Chinese were also the first really to exploit fully battened sails. The battens stopped the sail from fluttering or flogging, and helped to spread the load through the whole sail. This let the Chinese use woven mats in lieu of sailcloth, and if the makeshift sail ripped, the battens still allowed it to set and catch the wind, because the damage was limited to a single panel. We will see how all these features are still retained by the Western version of the rig.

The earliest recorded use of the junk rig by a 'Westerner' on a small boat was by Captain Joshua Slocum. Slocum is best remembered for his circumnavigation aboard *Spray*, but before that he was a commercial seaman. It was on one of his many commercial voyages that he was shipwrecked in South America, in 1888. His wife and two children had been with him on the ship, and he was now faced with getting them back to the United States, so he decided to build a small boat to do this, and the boat that he built was the thirty-five-foot *Liberdade*.

He designed and built the hull based on his 'recollections of a Cape Anne dory', and when it came to designing and building the rig for the boat, he used a photograph of a 'Chinese Sampan', whose rig he called 'the most convenient small-boat rig in the world'.

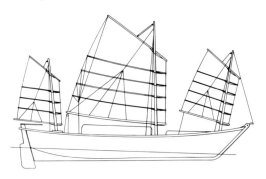

30. Slocum's *Liberdade*.

With his three-masted junk-rigged vessel, he carried his family to safety, covering almost 6,000 miles, spending only thirty-five days at sea. This was a remarkable achievement, but it was to be almost another seventy years before the potential of the junk rig for a small boat was to be fully realised.

In 1960, the ever inventive Colonel 'Blondie' Hasler was experimenting with rigs for his twenty-five foot Folkboat *Jester*. He had spent several years experimenting with a modified Ljungstrom rig which he called the Lapwing. This was a double sail which was reefed by wrapping it round the mast. He could not get the reefing system to work to his satisfaction—there was a tendency for the wind to get into the furled part of the sail, and cause it to start flapping. He finally abandoned the rig and took to experimenting with a Chinese lugsail.

This rig immediately showed great promise, and four months later Hasler and *Jester* were competing in the Single-handed Transatlantic Race using a single junk sail. Since then *Jester* has crossed the Atlantic twelve more times, mostly under the guidance of her present owner, Michael Richey, who has entered her in every OSTAR since that first one. A lot of miles for a little boat, and all with substantially the same rig.

Hasler teamed up with Jock McLeod in 1963, and together they worked at developing and refining the rig. In 1967 they drew the rig for Commander Bill King's *Galway Blazer II*, and in 1971, Jock launched his own *Ron Glas*, in which he has crossed the Atlantic six times without mishap. He gained some notoriety amongst his fellow OSTAR competitors by boasting that he was able to complete the race without ever having to change out of his carpet slippers, or to go on deck. Like *Jester*, his own boat has an inside control position where all sailhandling can be done without venturing outside.

The following year saw the rig first fitted to a production glassfibre hull. Rear Admiral R. L. Fisher was seeking an easily handled boat, and selected the junk rig to be fitted to his Kingfisher 30, *Yeong*. With this boat Admiral Fisher and his wife, without the benefit of additional crew, made a number of successful cruises, including a circumnavigation of Ireland when they were both rapidly approaching eighty years of age. The boat was so successful that Kingfisher went on to offer the junk rig as an option on their production twenty- and twenty-six-footers, and then slowly other builders followed suit as the rig began to gain acceptance.

The first junk-rigged boat that we ever sailed on was a Kingfisher 20, which was sailing in the first Mini-Transat. This is a singlehanded race from England to the Canaries, then on to Antigua, for boats under twenty-two feet. We met the fleet in the Canaries, and there was much wound licking going on. The competitors had been plagued by a series of fronts and depressions all the way out from England. What had upset a lot of people was that the little Kingfisher, complete with its twin keels, had beaten almost all of the hot stripped-out racers. In the constantly changing conditions the ability to reef and unreef without effort had allowed the boat to be kept sailing at her optimum speed. The livelier racing boats had worn their crews out, and consequently were sailed much slower. We got a short sail on the boat in exchange for scrubbing the bottom before the next leg of the race.

In 1977, Sunbird Yachts introduced the first production boat specifically designed for the junk rig, the Sunbird 32. This boat has been built with a single-masted junk rig, a schooner junk version, and for the unconverted, a Bermudan sloop version. Sunbird also undertake a design and conversion service to re-rig existing boats with the junk rig.

Newbridge Boats are also currently building production boats with the junk rig. Their range of boats up to twenty-

31. Junk-rigged schooner, Sunbird 32.

three feet has become very popular, and they sell almost as many junk-rigged boats as they do Bermudan.

On the American side of the Atlantic, various builders have offered Angus Primrose's North Atlantic 29 from time to time. This boat is really a big *Jester*, but has never really received wide acclaim.

The other junk-rig designer whose work is a little more common in the States is Tom Colvin. Unfortunately, many of his designs have been executed as heavy steel vessels, often with great beam and shallow draught. None of these factors has helped the sailing performance of these craft, and many people have been put off the rig by watching these boats sail. I am sure that these designs have their own attributes, but it appears that speed under sail is not one of them.

Understanding the Western Junk Rig

As mentioned earlier, there are many variations among traditional junks, which would make a fascinating study, but this is neither the time nor the place. For the purposes of this discussion we will confine ourselves largely to the rig as developed by Hasler and McLeod. There are more boats sailing successfully with variations of their rig than any other 'Western' junk rig, and Jock McLeod publishes extensive material for anybody wishing to benefit from their continuing experiments.

One of the most obvious departures from the so-called conventional rig that most junk rigs exhibit is the lack of standing rigging. On most junk-rigged boats of the size that we are interested in the masts are free standing. The first question that just about everybody asks is, why?

The simple answer is that standing rigging is not needed for a junk rig. On a Bermudan-rigged vessel, that big headsail needs a tight forestay for it to be set on. The tight forestay needs a tight backstay if the mast is not to fall over the bow. As soon as we have these two tight wires, then we must support the mast sideways, otherwise if it bends a little, the compressive load on the mast caused by these tight stays will make it collapse. As soon as we get rid of the headsail and the tight forestay the need for standing rigging vanishes. The fact that the junk sail is balanced, and the sheet load is spread along the entire leech of the sail, reduces the stress on any one point of the mast to a minimum. If we did want to put standing rigging on the mast, it could go only to the top. Since the sail itself touches the mast along most of its length we could not attach shrouds part way up, as is done with the Bermudan rig. We have already seen that the loading of the sail is spread over the whole mast, so there is no point in putting stays to just the masthead, where there is no particular concentration of stress, indeed such a localised restraining force may even endanger the mast.

To unaccustomed eyes the junk rig looks very complicated. In fact, when the rig is reduced to its component parts it is incredibly simple. Let's take a look at the nomenclature of the rig first.

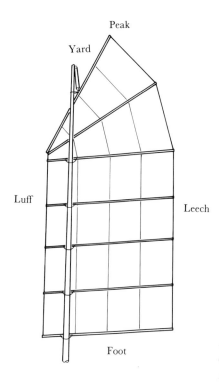

32. Junk sail showing names of parts of the sail.

Naming the parts of the sail is easy—they are named more or less in the same way as their Western counterparts.

When we come to rig the sail we are faced with a seemingly complex array of ropes, some of which have strange-sounding names. However, if we can look at each line in turn, and understand its purpose, then hopefully the parts will come together, if I dare say it, like the parts of a Chinese puzzle.

Just like almost every other, the junk sail is hoisted by a halyard, but because the full-length battens, and the yard which supports the top of the sail, make the sail heavy, the halyard is usually a three- or four-part purchase. Using such a purchase not only reduces the effort needed for hoisting the heavy sail, but it reduces the compressive loading on the mast. With a single-part halyard, the pull on the fall is the same as the weight of the sail, but with a purchase of four to one, the pull will be reduced to about one quarter of the weight. It would be possible to use a single-part halyard with a winch, but the extra pull on the fall of the halyard would add considerably to the compression. If too much load is put on the halyard, it would be similar to having a tight forestay and backstay with no lateral support. As soon as the mast bent a little, the tight fall of the halyard would act like the string on a bow, and it would make the mast bend more, perhaps until it broke. So if we are to have an unstayed mast with any rig, the compressive loads must be kept to a minimum.

Getting back to the halyard, it is attached to the centre of the yard, and is used for raising and lowering it. When the sail is fully hoisted, since the halyard has a three- or four-to-one purchase, its tail will be very long. It is a good idea to make some provision for stowing this long tail, either in a special locker or bin, or by rolling it up onto a special stowage reel, otherwise, as we very quickly found, the cockpit gets to look like a spaghetti factory.

The Chinese often resort to the use of several halyards to get the yard to set at the right angle. The Western version has an easier solution. There is another line that runs from the centre of the yard, and passes around the mast, back through a block on the yard, then down to the deck. This line is called the yard hauling parrel, and as its name suggests, it hauls the yard tight into the mast to get it to 'peak up' and set at the right angle.

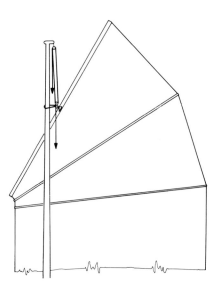

33. Halyard and yard hauling parrel.

The other basic piece of running rigging on the junk sail is the sheet, which is rigged to trim all, or all but the uppermost, of the battens. This helps to reduce the twist of the sail. If the sheet were run through a block on the end of each batten, there would probably be too many parts to the purchase of the system. If a purchase greater than about six to

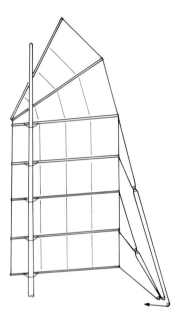

34. Sheet and span system.

one is used, there is too much friction, and the whole system becomes cumbersome to use, so the usual way is to run a span between adjacent battens, and by using a sister block on each span, sheet each pair of battens.

There are various other control lines that may or may not be used on a particular sail. The most common is the running luff parrel, which as its name suggests, helps to control the luff of the sail. It runs from the deck, up the mast to a block on the front of one of the battens. It then goes around the mast and up through a block on the front of the next batten. From there it goes around the mast once more to be fastened to the front of the next batten.

74

35. Running luff parrel—note that it does not make a spiral round the mast.

It is usually sufficient to have the parrel run to just the top three of the horizontal battens. It is used to help the set of the full sail, when the sail is tightened and thus pulled bodily back against the thrust of the yard, and it can help to remove creases from the sail. When reefing the sail, the running luff parrel pulls down the front of the upper battens, and helps to keep the luff tight.

If the running luff parrel is not fitted, then it may be necessary to use downhauls to the front of the battens to hold them down when reefing. By fitting a span between adjacent battens, one downhaul can pull down two battens.

When rigging our boat, we made provision for fitting

downhauls, but we have never found a need for them, thanks to the running luff parrel, so have not fitted them. Using a single running luff parrel instead of multiple downhauls helps to keep the numbers of control lines down.

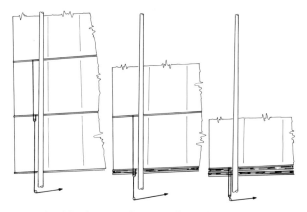

36. Downhaul fitted to a span between adjacent battens—showing how each batten in turn is pulled down as the sail is reefed.

Sailing the Junk Rig

Using the rig is really very easy. The first thing to remember is that the halyard works against all the other running rigging, so when the sail is being hoisted, the sheet, the yard hauling parrel and the running luff parrel or any downhauls must be slackened off and allowed to run free. Because of the weight of the sail, battens and yard, hoisting the sail is quite a healthy exercise. But with a multi-part halyard, winches are not really needed on sails up to about five hundred square feet. However for those people with a strong aversion to exercise, a self tailing, or even an electric winch can make for very lazy sailing. Even if a winch is used, remember the need to reduce the compression on the mast, and do not be tempted to go to a single-part halyard to reduce the amount of rope.

76

It is easiest to hoist the sail with the wind foreward of the beam, so that it does not fill. As soon as one begins to hoist the sail, the advantage of the fully battened sail becomes apparent. There is no flapping of the sail, and with the sheet slack it will lie quietly, weathercocking into the wind, leaving you all the time in the world to set up the rest of the control lines.

Once the halyard is secured, the yard hauling parrel is pulled tight to peak up the yard, and if there is a running luff parrel fitted, it too is pulled tight to remove any creases in the sail. All that remains is to trim the sheet and away you go. Not too complicated, really.

When hoisting the sail, it is not necessary to hoist it all to begin with. If the wind is very strong, then hoist only sufficient panels to give you the required amount of sail area. Even in more moderate winds, it might be advantageous to start off with a reduced amount of sail. For example, if sailing off an anchor, it may be worth starting with perhaps half the sail area set, then one can manoeuvre clear of the other boats at half throttle, as it were. Once ready to set full sail, slacken off the sheet, yard hauling parrel and the running luff parrel and any downhauls, then pull the halyard up the rest of the way, tighten up the parrels and away you go.

Reefing is equally easy. It is a case of slackening away on the halyard until the required number of panels are reefed down, then re-tightening the parrels. There is a system of lazy jacks that hold the reefed portion of the sail on top of the boom. The mainsheet holds down the after ends of the reefed battens, and the running luff parrel or the downhauls hold down the forward ends. There is no need to tie in any reef points, and if all the control lines are led to the cockpit, there is no need to go on deck. With a junk-rigged boat, the only time that you might want to change sails would be if you wanted to set a light-weather drifter, otherwise, the working sails will reef for all other conditions. It is usual for junk-rigged sails to accommodate four or five reefs, which makes it very easy to adjust the sail area to the prevailing conditions.

Reefing and unreefing are best done with the wind forward of the beam and the sail feathering. However, since there is no standing rigging for the sail to chafe on or press against, it is possible to reef or unreef a junk sail on a dead run. When doing this, though, you must take great care not to let the sail swing forward of the beam, because as the sail comes down, the sheet effectively becomes longer, and the sail will swing out further. If the sail is allowed to swing forward of the beam, it is likely that the battens will break. With the sail out abeam, the sheet just exerts a bending stress on the battens, which they should be able to take. However, if the sail is forward of the beam, and if the sheet is pulled in to try and bring it back, the pull of the sheet will put a compressive load on the battens. If the battens are bending at all, and they are then subjected to such an additional force, it is likely that they will break.

If the sail is accidentally allowed into this position, the temptation to pull on the sheet must be resisted. The boat should be turned to bring the wind forward of the beam, when the sail will swing back by itself. Once the pressure is off the sail, the sheet can be safely tightened.

The actual technique of sailing with a junk rig is quite simple, but it does take some practice to get the best out of the rig. The first junk-rigged boat that I ever saw in action was a genuine Hong Kong junk. She had been built for one of the Panama Canal pilots, called Hank, and he had had her shipped out to the Canal Zone to be used as a family cruising boat. Much to his dismay, she sailed like a dog, she could hardly get out of her own way. In a fit of pique he telephoned the builders and they agreed to fly somebody over to see what the problem was. About a week later your archetypal Chinaman, complete with pigtail, stepped off the

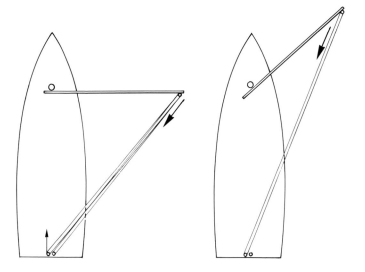

37. Showing bending load on battens with the sail abeam, and compressive
load with the sail forward of the beam.

plane, and proceeded to tweak and adjust all the lines on the
boat. The following day he took everybody out for a sail.
The old girl was transformed, she sailed like a witch, and
Hank thought all his troubles were over and bought everybody a beer.

The next weekend, after our oriental visitor had returned
to the East, Hank invited everybody out for a sail. You've
guessed it, the old tug sailed worse than ever without the
oriental touch on the helm.

The fully battened sails do not readily indicate poor trim.
It is very easy to get the boat to sail, but, as Hank found out,
and we rediscovered when we launched our own boat, it
takes a definite technique to get the rig to go well.

The easiest mistake to make when sailing to windward is

to trim the sails in too tight. The sails must be eased out a lot more than on a Bermudan-rigged boat, and the boat sailed perhaps a little freer. It would appear that the flat sails must be set at a much smaller angle of attack to the wind than conventional sails.

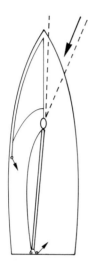

38. Showing angle of attack for Bermudan sail and for a flat junk sail—both sails trimmed for going to windward.

In calm water, on a good hull, a junk rig should be able to tack through 90 degrees. However, into much of a sea, the flat sails seem to lack the drive to push through the waves. Under these conditions it will be necessary to fall off a little, and the tacking angle will be about 110 to 115 degrees. For most cruising boats this should be acceptable. Falling off that 10 degrees or so usually results in a motion that is kinder to both boat and crew. The flexibility of an unstayed rig tends to absorb the shocks somewhat when going to windward, so although the junk-rigged boat may take a little longer than a Bermudan boat on a passage to windward, the crew are likely to arrive in a better state.

In 1974 I was in Crosshaven, Ireland, when the fleet arrived at the end of a tempestuous first leg of the two-handed Round Britain and Ireland Race. The local sail-makers were having a field day, repairing damage sustained on the long hard beat. There was much wound licking going on.

There were two junk-rigged boats in the fleet, Jock McLeod with *Ron Glas*, and *Galway Blazer* that had recently been bought by Peter Crowther. Admittedly they were not up with the front runners, but they arrived with a conspicuous lack of problems that needed solving. Jock's crew was telling everybody about the soccer match he had been watching on T.V. on the way over, and Peter's crew was desperate to swop some books, as he had read all the good ones on board, and they still had a couple of weeks of racing to go.

The contrast between these four, and the rest of the crews was striking. I spent that evening in the bar with Jock, and ordered his junk-rig design folios there and then, even though it was several years before I got round to building the next boat.

Under very changeable conditions, or when short tacking up a narrow channel, the junk-rigged vessel is usually more than able to hold her own. As the strength of the wind varies, the junk rig is so easy to reef and unreef it is easy to keep the boat sailing near her optimum. By contrast, to keep a Bermudan-rigged boat sailing at her best it is likely that there will have to be several sail changes made, all of which will take some time and will involve people being up on deck.

A few years ago, we raced our own thirty-five foot junk-rigged schooner in the anual 'Sweethearts of the Caribbean' schooner race, in the Virgin Islands. We were one of the smallest boats in the race, which was raced boat for boat, no handicaps, just divided into under and over sixty feet. They only let us sail in the Traditional class after we had pointed out that the junk rig is at least two thousand years older than this new-fangled gaff rig that they kept going on about. We were rather overcrewed for the race, as two friends had asked to come along. Since one got drunk, and the other fell asleep before the start, Lana and I could sail the boat how we pleased.

It was one of those days when squall after squall came through, and since each squall was of only about ten minutes' duration, most of the boats had to decide whether to be overpressed in the squalls, or under-canvassed in the lulls. We reefed and unreefed for every squall, and we must have had close to a dozen squalls in the course of the three-hour race, and kept the boat sailing at her best, despite the enthusiastic help from our inebriated friend.

We got second place, close behind a beautiful fifty-eight-foot Alden schooner that had just about exhausted her numerous and enthusiastic crew. Because we could easily keep the right amount of sail area set, we beat many much larger boats which, I will be the first to admit, would have thrashed us in steadier conditions. So whilst the junk rig may not be the fastest rig in the world, it is not too strenuous to keep the boat sailing at her best.

Likewise, short tacking a boat with a self-tending rig, particularly one with fully battened sails, is an absolute joy. Tacking is just a case of putting the tiller over, and settling down on the new course. There is no winching to be done, nor are there any flapping sails. The sails just swing over gently and quietly, until they fill on the new tack.

While sailing our boat we have enjoyed many an impromptu race, often against much faster Bermudan-rigged boats. We always try and lure them into a tacking duel, and we wait until they have just sheeted the genoa home before giving them a sweet smile and putting the tiller over to tack again. The effect is heightened if both of us keep a drink in hand during the manoeuvre, and after the second tack, we can almost feel the glares. After the third or fourth tack in as many minutes they almost always give up in disgust.

Another big advantage with the junk rig if beating in confined waters is that there is no headsail to get caught aback. It is unnerving, to say the least, to be sailing a Bermudan boat in a tight situation, and be pinching up close to the wind, when suddenly the wind shifts a little and the jib is caught aback. Often there is no time to release the sheet before the backed jib forces the head round, and you have tacked, whether there was room to do so or not. With a self-tending rig such as the junk rig, this cannot happen. If you are pinching up and the wind comes round a bit, all that will happen is that the sails will feather into the wind and the boat will slow down. There is lots of time to decide whether to bear away and continue sailing on the same tack, or if it would indeed be better to tack. Either way, you are able to make the choice. So under short tacking conditions, a junk-rigged vessel will not only be much easier, but it will also be much safer to sail in confined waters, and certainly life will be much easier for the crew.

When we first built our present boat, we didn't have (couldn't afford) an engine, except for a somewhat recalcitrant outboard. After leaving England in the middle of winter, our first landfall was Wicklow, on the east coast of Ireland. We crept into the outer harbour soon after midnight on a very cold and dark night. At dawn, we decided to move to a more sheltered berth up the river, next to a not very picturesque fertilizer factory, since a northerly gale was forecast, and our present anchorage would become uncomfortable at best.

Try as we might, the outboard would not start. Since it was Sunday, it obviously thought that it deserved a day of rest. We cleaned the plug and even warmed it up in the oven. We wiped out the carburettor and tried fresh fuel, all to no avail. There was just a gentle breeze blowing, but unfortunately it was coming smack down the centre of the river. We decided to have a go at beating up the river anyway, and hoisted the sails.

The banks of the river are steep to, which was just as well since the river was only about four or five boat lengths wide. One tack took us literally within about three feet of the road. A car screeched to a halt next to us, and the driver, who was close enough for us to touch, stuck his head out of the window, and in a rich Irish brogue asked, 'Is that strictly necessary?' We assured him that it was and tacked over towards the fertilizer factory again.

It must have taken us near on fifty tacks to make that hundred yards up the river, but we made it, and at least in retrospect, actually enjoyed doing it. The exercise certainly taught us how our boat handled in confined quarters.

It is off the wind, though, that a junk-rigged boat really comes into her own. Because the flat sails are set at a smaller angle of attack to the wind, they do not press the boat as much as a Bermudan sail. Junk-rigged boats will commonly sail much more upright on a reach than other boats.

If the wind is on, or forward of the beam, it is often unnecessary to reef for a squall. The sheet can be eased out a little, the sail set at an even finer angle of attack, which will reduce the pressing effect. Indeed, with the wind on or forward of the beam, it is possible to let the sheet fly completely. The sail will swing out and lie quietly feathering into the wind. The battens stop it from flogging or flapping about. This can be very useful at meal times, or when struggling to take a bearing, a sight, or just trying to go to the head. The advantage of simply being able to stop for a few moments, and then get going again without a great deal of effort should not be underestimated.

Because the flat sails are set at a fine angle of attack to the wind, and the full-length battens stop them from flogging, junk-rigged sails perform exceptionally well when motor-sailing. We have found that, when sheeted in amidships, they will still generate some lift at only about fifteen to twenty degrees off the true wind. There is not enough lift generated for the boat to sail herself this close to the wind, but when motor-sailing, the boat will be steadier and going faster than if just under motor alone. It is possible, under light conditions, to tack through thirty to forty degrees on the compass, making better speed than under motor alone. It is not possible to motor-sail this close to the wind with a Bermudan-rigged boat, as the sails would be flogging themselves to destruction.

Conclusions

The junk rig already has the reputation of being one of the easiest rigs to reef. Unless one wants to set light-weather sails, there is no need to change sails, and it is easy to arrange all reefing and unreefing from the cockpit.

We have found this to be invaluable when making long passages on our own boat with just the two of us on board. In changing conditions either one of us can reef or unreef the sails without disturbing the person off watch to come and help. I seem to sleep that much better knowing that there is little chance that I will be woken up part way through my off watch to go and help reef, and I also rest easier knowing that if there is a sudden squall, it will take Lana but a few seconds to reef down safely, and she will not be prancing around on deck risking a trip over the side.

When we crossed Biscay, we sailed very conservatively, for the boat was new and as yet untried. We reefed for every squall, and sometimes for every cloud. It was a particularly cold and boisterous April, and we thanked the rig every time that we reefed down from the shelter of the companionway. Although we did get some bad weather, and it was very cold, neither of us got particularly tired, and we both commented afterwards how nice and dry the boat stayed, but then we hadn't dragged any wet sails through the accommodation. Despite the inclement weather, it was actually an easier passage than our two previous crossings, both of which had been on larger boats.

The rig is quite unsophisticated, there is little or no expensive hardware required. This makes the junk one of the easiest rigs for home construction. Even the flat sails are very easy to make, I made ours on Mother-in-Law's sewing machine. There is little on the rig that can fail, but should anything break, it is pretty much 'fail safe'. For example, should the halyard part, the sail will drop, and more or less stow itself in the lazy jacks. Should the sheet carry away, the sail will swing round until it feathers into the wind, where it will lie quietly. The battens will stop it from flogging itself to destruction. Should the sail itself tear, the damage is likely to be limited to the area between adjacent battens. If cringles are fitted above and below each batten, the damaged panel can be reefed out by tying the two adjacent battens together. Indeed a broken batten can be similarly lashed to its neighbour until a replacement can be fitted. If the sail is made with vertical seams, should the stiching fail and a seam split, it will go only between battens, rather than right across. The battens will stop the sail from flapping about, and it is likely that you will be able to continue sailing on with no difficulty. If it does cause a problem, then again the two battens can be tied together to reef out the damaged area.

The rig is good for shorthanded sailing, and for motor-sailing, and the ability to put in or take out usually four or five reefs per sail with little effort, and without leaving the cockpit, makes for a rig that can be easily sailed at its optimum under changing conditions without changing sails.

The only shortcoming of the rig is the windward performance in anything but very smooth seas. The rig is not as fast to windward as an equivalent Bermudan boat, but the passage is likely to be easier on the crew aboard the junk-rigged vessel. Many people, including ourselves, have found the windward performance to be adequate, if not exactly sparkling, and for us, the other benefits outweigh this shortcoming. For others, windward performance is everything, being more important even than the comfort and safety of the crew.

No doubt our boat would be faster if we put on some more efficient sails, but we are too firmly hooked on the self-tending and reefing aspects of the junk to go back to a Bermudan rig. After having sailed the boat getting on for ten thousand miles without any problems (touching wood furiously as I write that), we are reluctant to change anything, and loath to move away from the absolute simplicity of the junk rig. There are, however, several rigs that have been developed from the junk rig. They offer increased performance, yet hopefully still retain all the attributes of the junk rig. Let's move on and consider a couple of these rigs.

5

Rigs Developed from the Junk
—Swing Wing and Gallant

We have just seen that the junk rig certainly has its merits, especially when it comes to reefing. However, there are those who feel that the less than racing performance to windward is not acceptable. Some people are sufficiently enamoured with the concept of the junk rig that they have expended considerable effort trying to improve the windward capabilities without losing the easy reefing and handling benefits of the rig.

We will take a look at two of these developments, the Swing Wing and the Gallant rigs, as representative of the work that is going on. They are very different in concept, yet they are both trying to achieve the same objective, namely putting an aerofoil shape into the otherwise flat junk sail.

The Swing Wing Rig

The Swing Wing looks a lot like the junk rig, from which it was developed. This is not surprising, because it is the brainchild of the Sunbird Yacht company, who built the first production boat designed specifically for junk rig, the Sunbird 32.

The way this rig strives to achieve an efficient aerofoil is to use articulated battens. The battens themselves look somewhat like a tadpole, with the tail being the part that articulates or swings. Each batten is fabricated from three pieces of very stiff alloy tube, with the forward two pieces being bent to form the wishbone shape.

The forward two thirds of the sail is double, and encloses

88

39. Westerly Centaur fitted with a single-masted Swing Wing rig.

40. Swing Wing batten.

41. Westerly Centaur with Sunbird's Swing Wing rig.

the mast. This helps to get a good airflow over the sail, and eliminates the turbulence that the mast of the junk rig causes. The after third of the sail is single ply, and is supported by the articulating tail of each batten.

The sail still effectively has full-length battens, so it can feather into the wind without flogging, just like the junk sail. However, as soon as it is sheeted in, the wind in the sails causes the battens to hinge at the joint, and the sail assumes a fairly efficient aerofoil shape. On a change of tack, the battens will of course hinge the other way, and again form the aerofoil shape.

The shape of the forward section of the sail is controlled by the wishbone part of the battens. The aerofoil shape is governed largely by how far the battens are allowed to swing. Stops are built into the battens to limit the degree of swing to where the straight part of the sail continues the line of the lee side of the sail.

The sheeting system of the junk rig is retained, with a sheetlet between each pair of battens, and a multi-part sheet running through blocks on each sheetlet. Such a sheeting system helps to spread the load throughout the sail, and by sheeting all the way up the leech, twist in the sail is reduced.

We sailed on a Sunbird 32 with the prototype Swing Wing rig, out of the Hamble River. As soon as we started sailing to windward, we noticed that only the lower two or three battens actually hinged as far as their stops allowed. The higher battens hinged part way, but not against their stops. This perhaps shows how evenly the loads are spread through the sail, and suggests that the hinges, which might appear to be a weak point, are not in fact very highly stressed at all.

As for sailhandling and reefing, the Swing Wing seems to have retained all the good points from the junk rig. Hoisting the sail is easy. The sail would appear to be about the same weight as the equivalent size junk-rigged sail. The battens are a little heavier, but there is no yard on the Swing Wing. To make it easier to hoist the rather heavy sail, and to reduce compression on the unstayed mast, a multi-part halyard is used, similar to that used on the junk rig. The hoisted sail will lie feathering into the wind without flogging. The battens tend to swing to one side, and lie there quietly. They did not appear to want to keep hingeing to and fro when feathering.

Reefing is entirely comparable to the junk rig. To reef, the halyard is slackened off until the required number of panels are lowered. The multi-part sheet takes care of holding down the after ends of the reefed battens, while a system of downhauls holds down the forward ends and keeps the luff of the sail reasonably taut. An arrangement of lazy jacks, again identical to those used on the junk rig, holds the lowered battens and panels of sail in place. There is no need to tie in reef points, or to go on deck at all when reefing, nor indeed when lowering the sail.

So how well does the rig sail? Compared to the junk rig, there is no doubt at all that to windward, or even on a very close reach, it is superior. Most of Sunbird's work has been purely empirical. They have been using a Laser dinghy as a floating test bed for various rigs. According to their tests on the Laser, the Swing Wing is now as efficient to windward as the normal Bermudan-rigged Laser sail. However, the windward performance is still not going to be the same as a Bermudan-rigged boat with a deck-sweeping genoa and an army of gorillas to tame it. However, we did enjoy being able to short-tack back up the river at the end of the day, when everybody else was motoring. It was no problem to tack every fifty yards or so, with no sheets to tend, and we were consistently tacking through ninety degrees on the compass. A very satisfying end to an interesting sail.

*　　　*　　　*

Compared to the junk rig, the Swing Wing offers improved windward performance, with similar easy reefing, and tacking without winching. It achieves this increase in performance because of the improved aerofoil shape of the sail, and thanks to the reduction of turbulence and windage caused by the mast, since the mast is enclosed within the sail.

It will cost a little more than the junk rig, since the doubled portion of the sail necessitates more sailcloth; and the battens are more complicated, which may mean buying them rather than making them. The hinges in the battens are an added complication, and perhaps added weak points.

Nonetheless, they do appear to be very lightly loaded in use, and it should be entirely possible to make them strong enough to withstand anything that the rest of the batten will.

Compared to a Bermudan-rigged boat, the Swing Wing offers much easier reefing, without venturing on deck, tacking without winching, and sails which will feather into the wind without flogging. The rig is good also for motor-sailing, since the sails do not flog if one pinches up a bit too close to the wind. The cost should be comparable to a Bermudan rig, since although the rig itself is a bit more complicated, there is no standing rigging, nor are there big expensive winches to buy. The rig is very forgiving to sail, trim is not terribly critical unless one is searching for the last tiny bit of performance. It is very easy to sail quite well with the rig, and there is no possibility of being caught aback in a tight situation. The rig fails safe. If anything were to break, the sail will either feather into the wind, or will lower and effectively stow itself. There is no chance of suddenly ending up with more sail set than you want.

To the uninitiated, the rig appears more complicated than a simple Bermudan rig, but actually, once the function of each line is understood, it is a very simple rig to use. The performance to windward is not that of a racing boat, but it is perfectly adequate for cruising. For my money, the ease of handling, and the safety of reefing from the cockpit, more than offsets this very slight reduction in performance.

The Gallant Rig
The Gallant rig, developed by Jack Manners-Spencer, does not have such a strong family resemblance to the junk rig, but it does share several of its characteristics. It has a fully battened sail set on an unstayed mast. This rig seeks a higher degree of aerodynamic efficiency than the junk rig by having a double-sided sail set on wishbone battens which give the sail an aerofoil shape. Like the Swing Wing, the

42. and 43 Jack Manners-Spencer's Gallant rig on the
Endurance 40, *Cameleon*.

mast is enclosed within the sail, which much reduces the drag. In profile the sails have an elliptical shape, which is a very efficient shape for a wing or sail. The traditional triangular shape of a sail is very inefficient, inasmuch as it causes considerable turbulence, which results in drag, at the tip. The elliptical shape much reduces this.

The general appearance of the sail reminds one of a Spitfire aircraft wing rather than a sail. This is not too surprising, given Jack Manners-Spencer's earlier career in the Royal Air Force.

The battens themselves are made from a specially extruded alloy section, which is curved to the wishbone shape. The sail is made up from a series of individual panels, each with a boltrope top and bottom, which slide into grooves in the extrusion.

This method of construction allows for easy removal and subsequent replacement of any individual panel that may get damaged. Any fully battened sail is heavy and cumbersome to remove from the mast to repair. It is certainly an advantage to be able to remove a single panel. Such a sail is

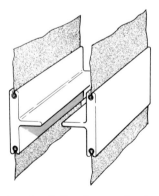

44. Section through a Gallant batten—showing sail panels fitting into batten.

probably also easier (and hence conceivably cheaper) to make, since the small individual panels are much more manageable than the whole sail to work on.

One of the aims for the Gallant rig has been to keep it as simple as possible. This has been achieved to the point where there are only two items of running rigging for each sail, the halyard and the sheet.

We sailed from Lymington aboard Jack Manners-Spencer's own boat, *Cameleon*. She is an Endurance 40 which he has fitted with the Gallant rig. She is obviously a much heavier boat than the Sunbird 32, so direct comparisons are difficult.

The sail is about the same weight as the Swing Wing, or the junk, so it is quite heavy to hoist. Again, to make life easier, and to reduce compression on the mast, a multi-part halyard is used, usually a purchase of 3:1 is sufficient. On his own boat, to make life even easier, Jack Manners-Spencer uses an electric winch for the halyards. By having a stopper for each halyard, one winch can serve both halyards on his schooner rig. With the 3:1 purchase, though, it was still entirely feasible to hoist the sails by hand.

Hoisting the sails is very straightforward, with only the halyard and the sheet to consider. The lowered sails lie in a bundle on top of the boom, restrained by the topping lifts, which double as lazy jacks. Like the junk, or the Swing Wing, it is easiest to hoist the sails with the wind forward of the beam. While hoisting, and when hoisted, the sails lie quietly feathering into the wind. To get under way, the sheet is hardened in, and here came the first surprise. The sheet was a single part, just one length of line coming off the end of the boom. We wondered how this could possibly control almost 500 square feet of sail area of the mainsail.

The secret is in the balance of the sails. The mast is so positioned that about one third of the sail area is forward of the mast, and about two thirds behind it. This has the effect of dramatically reducing the load on the sheet, and it also reduces the twist of the sails to negligible proportions.

The boat tacked through about 95 degrees, and appeared to foot quite well. Tacking was similar to the junk rig, and the Swing Wing, inasmuch as the sail swings across silently, without flapping, as the head of the boat passes through the wind. Going to windward, it is quite hard to tell when the boat is sailing at her best. However, like the Swing Wing, and for that matter the junk, the rig is very forgiving, and again, it is easy to make the rig sail quite well. Constant vigilance with the luff tell-tales is required to get the last little bit of speed.

We noticed that the aerofoil sails kept generating some lift even when we pinched up almost head to wind, so this could be the best rig yet for motor-sailing, which is a good way for any cruising boat to make to windward.

So far as reefing is concerned, Jack Manners-Spencer has opted for simplicity, rather than complete control from the cockpit. The basic reefing system is like the junk rig in that as you slacken away the halyard, the sail lowers itself panel by panel, to lie on top of the boom. Here Jack departs from the junk concept, because at this point he goes forward to cleat four little pendants from the topmost reefed batten to the boom. These pendants are permanently attached to each batten, one at each end, and one amidships on either side. His feeling is that this is easier than resorting to a complicated system of downhauls to hold down the battens. There is no doubt that a downhaul system could be rigged, but it would be much more complicated than on the Swing Wing or the junk rig, where in both cases the after end of the sail is held down by the multi-part sheet. The fastening off of the pendants is certainly much easier and safer than fighting on the foredeck, trying to change a headsail.

For light-weather reaching conditions, there have been experiments done on the Gallant rig with an additional 'flap sail'. This additional sail is hoisted on a halyard attached to usually the sixth batten, and it is tacked down part-way along the windward side of the boom. The clew is fastened to a short pole which is attached to the end of the boom. The idea of this sail is not to increase the area, but to improve the shape of the aerofoil. The flap sail is sheeted at about sixty degrees to the axis of the boom, and it works rather like the flaps on an aircraft wing when it is landing. It distorts the airflow over the aerofoil, and increases the lift. This is the same thing they are trying to achieve with the Swing Wing, but in the case of the Gallant, this extra sail must be taken down and reset on each tack.

Conclusions

Compared with a Bermudan boat, the pros and cons are similar to those put forward for the Swing Wing rig. So let's look at the differences between the Gallant and the Swing Wing.

Jack Manners-Spencer's approach to the Gallant rig has been rather more theoretical than Sunbird's with the Swing Wing, which is not to say that the Gallant has not been well proven at sea, because it has. The Gallant rig is designed to the NACA section 0015, which has been calculated to give a coefficient of lift some seventy per cent greater than that developed by the junk sail. No such figures were available for the Swing Wing, but in practice it would appear that both rigs seem to develop similar lift, with perhaps a slight edge to the Swing Wing in lighter conditions, and when reaching.

The Gallant rig has a very rounded leading edge to the sail, and this perhaps makes the sail less susceptible to stalling than the Swing Wing sail. Development on both rigs is still continuing, so by now, the Swing Wing could well have an improved leading edge. The section of the Gallant sail is symmetrical, which, whilst undoubtedly better than the flat sail of the junk, is far from ideal. By being able to articulate,

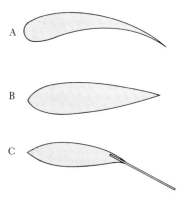

45. Comparing sections of A—Ideal aerofoil, B—Gallant rig,
C—Swing Wing.

the Swing Wing comes closer to approximating the ideal section.

As previously discussed, the Gallant can set the flap sail to improve the lift under reaching conditions, but for most people I feel that this will prove to be more trouble than it is worth.

The Gallant is apparently simpler than the Swing Wing, until one considers use of the flap sails. The Swing Wing, as conceived, lets one do all sailhandling from the cockpit, whereas the Gallant does require short forays on deck when reefing.

Both rigs show a considerable improvement over the junk when going to windward. Whether this increase in perform-ance is worth the extra cost and complication rather depends on the depth of one's purse, and the type of sailing one proposes to do.

The Swing Wing is aimed purely at the yacht market. Safety with reasonable performance is what they are looking for. The Gallant rig is being aimed at wider markets. As well as yachts, it is thought to be useful for work boats of various sorts, including fishing boats. With this in mind, simplicity is the keynote, since some of the potential users will have little interest in the finer points of sailing.

My choice for a small cruising boat, say up to about forty feet, would be the Swing Wing. The rig would be more expensive to build than the junk rig, but I think that the increase in performance probably warrants it. Sunbird is prepared to supply a kit of parts for the home builder who wishes to make his own rig.

The Gallant rig would perhaps be better for larger boats, since it is easier to build it stronger, with the rigid battens. This is one of the best rigs that we have seen for work boats, and perhaps one day soon we will see Gallant-rigged fishing boats. The simplicity of the rig, together with reasonable efficiency and the ability to lie feathered into the wind all would be useful to such a vessel. Both rigs are still developing, and I feel that the ultimate cruising rig will perhaps be a hybrid of these two.

In the United States, development of a rather different type of rig has been going on. This is similar to these rigs in that a single sail is set on each mast, and the masts are usually unstayed. The rig is the catboat rig, which at first glance looks somewhat like a conventional Bermudan rig, without the headsail. Let's now take a look at the history and development of this rig, and see how these boats fare without a headsail.

6

Catboats, and
the Freedom Development

Although their history does not stretch back into the mists of
time like that of the junks, catboats are nothing new. They
have been around for the last 150 years or so, and reached
the height of their popularity around the turn of the century.

The development of the catboat has been peculiarly
American, and limited largely to the North-Eastern parts of
the States. The rig was developed in working boats, primarily shoal-draught fishing boats, many of which were
built with centreboards to give them the shallow draught
needed. To get the required stability, the boats became quite
beamy, often the beam was as much as half of the length.

Their rig was developed to cope with local conditions. In
the summer there tended to be fairly light winds most of the
time, but the winters were predominantly rougher and
windier. Because of these two disparate conditions, many of
the boats were designed to carry two completely different
rigs. The summer rig was a fairly conventional sloop rig,
with a gaff main and a jib set on a bowsprit. The winter rig
was the cat rig. The mast was restepped further forward,
and the boat sailed with a single gaff sail, as it was felt that
this was a safer rig in heavy conditions. The boat had less
sail area for the stronger winds, and it was all inboard, so
nobody had to work out on the end of the bowsprit trying to
tame a flogging jib.

By about 1870 the catboat had become quite well established, and boats other than workboats began to appear
with the rig. Racing classes were started specifically for cat-

boats, and so-called party boats, built to take groups out fishing for pleasure, were built with the cat rig.

Traditionally the catboats had a large single sail, set on a mast that was often unstayed, or had just a forestay. Almost without exception the sails were gaff-rigged. Some boats sported a running bowsprit that could be run out to set a jib when conditions were favourable. The materials available at this time effectively limited the size of a single-masted catboat to about forty-five feet. Towards the end of the nineteenth century a few larger catboats, including a few pilot boats were built, but they were built with two masts.

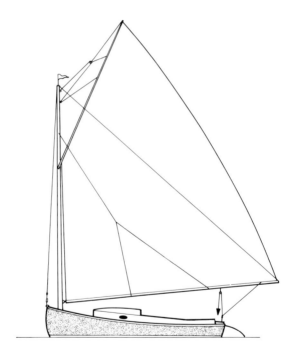

46. Typical traditional American catboat. (Note lazy jacks.)

As we progressed into the twentieth century, the popularity of the rig began to wane. One or two people continued
to build catboats, and lots more were still sailing them, particularly on the North-Eastern seaboard of the United
States. However the rig did not stage its renaissance until
one-time advertising executive Garry Hoyt launched the
Freedom range, with his Freedom 40. I suspect that it is partially Hoyt's advertising background, but it is also the way
that he has adapted modern materials that has led to the
success of the Freedoms and the resurgence of the cat rig:
many people now refer to a cat rig as the Freedom rig.

We will follow the development of the Freedom rig as
being typical of modern catboat development. We will look
at how the rig has changed since that first Freedom 40 started everybody talking anew about catboats.

When he launched that first Freedom 40, Hoyt was not
even re-inventing the wheel, all he was really doing was
publicising what a good invention it was. There was nothing
particularly innovative about his boat. The Herreshoff-
designed hull was quite beamy, and sported a centreboard
in true catboat tradition. The rig consisted of two aluminium lamp posts for masts, with wrap-around, double-
sided sails. Instead of conventional booms, Hoyt used
wishbone booms, angled downwards to keep the leech of the
sail tight without resorting to a kicking strap or vang. None
of this was new, except perhaps the aluminium lamp posts.
Bermudan-rigged catboats, although not traditional, were
already in existence, and wishbone booms have been around
for a while.

What was new was Garry Hoyt daring to thumb his nose
at the Establishment and say 'enough of this nonsense'. He
loudly queried the need for deck-sweeping genoas, and the
crew and complications that go with them, on a cruising
boat. He then took his Freedom 40 and proceeded to thrash
many racier cousins on the race course. Suddenly he was in

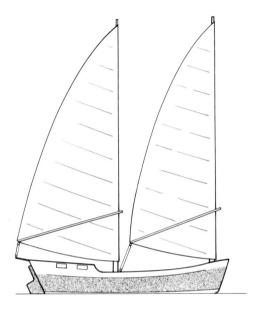

47. The boat that started the revolution—Freedom 40.

the limelight, and everybody was talking about the Freedom rig.

Far from resting on his laurels, Hoyt set about refining and marketing his product, both of which he has done admirably. Eight years later the basic wrap-around sail version is still available from Freedom, and other manufacturers, although as we shall see, Freedom offer two other alternative rigs. The original Freedom 40 is still sailing with her lamp posts, but the production boats switched to glass-and-carbon-fibre composite masts, then to the current all carbon-fibre masts. We will look at the structure of the masts in detail in the last chapter.

48. and 49. Garry Hoyt's Freedom 40 catboat.

Freedoms, and many of the other modern catboats, are offered with one of three basic rigs within the catboat concept. There is the original Freedom rig, with the wrap-around double sail, set with wishbone booms. Then there are the single-ply sails set on a conventional boom. Such sails are sometimes fully battened, but they need not be. Finally, in the quest for even higher performance, there are the rotating wing masts, which are almost always used in conjunction with fully battened sails.

In this chapter we will concentrate on the first two variations, and then look at wing spars and some of the other more esoteric rigs in the next chapter.

Catboat Rigs With Wrap-around Sails

The obvious first question is why would one want to use wrap-around sails at all? The answer is that such a sail actually makes a very efficient aerofoil shape, and since the mast is enclosed within the sail, turbulence and drag are reduced to a minimum.

50. Section through wrap-around sail, enclosed within the wishbone boom.

In the early days of unstayed masts, made of solid wood, or the ubiquitous alloy lamp posts, the diameter of the mast was considerable. If the mast was not enclosed within the leading edge of the sail, the drag and the turbulence caused by the mast would be unacceptably high. Now with modern materials, such as carbon fibre, the diameter of a freestanding mast can be reduced to where it does not cause undue turbulence in front of the sail. This is perhaps one reason why we see fewer wrap-around sails being used now, compared to a few years ago.

We were fortunate enough to sail on the original Freedom 40, long after Garry Hoyt had sold her. She still had her original lamp posts and her original sails. We found that the friction of the sail on the mast and the weight of the hefty wishbones made hoisting the sails a healthy exercise. But once the sails were set, sailing the boat was effortless. Tacking and gybing was every bit as easy as with the junk rig. No winching to do! When tacking, the sails did flap about somewhat, and rattle the wishbones, so it was not as quiet as with fully battened sails.

There is no doubt that the boat sails extremely well, as all those people that Hoyt has beaten when racing will testify. She certainly went to windward better than our junk rig, and on a par with most of the cruising boats that were out that day.

When we came to try reefing the wrap-around sails we found that it was not the easiest, and certainly a lot more difficult than our own boat. To be fair though, the boat we were sailing on had the earliest system, and reefing her sails involved lowering the wishbone to horizontal, pulling down the luff of the sail, tightening the pendant to the leech, then tying up the loose sail into the wishbone. Not a task to be undertaken lightly. Even then, only one reef in each sail was possible.

On later boats, the system is much improved. The wishbone stays in place, and a continuous reefing line tightens the luff and leech simultaneously. The loose part of the sail is drawn down into the lower part of the sail. Using this system, it is possible to put two reefs in each sail. This system is fine in theory, but it has some drawbacks in practice. The biggest is the friction of the sail on the mast. When the sail is wet, it tends to stick to the mast, making it very hard to pull the sail up or down.

Even when the sail was being lowered, it did not come down too easily. It tended to bunch up around the mast, requiring somebody to be at the mast to help the sail down. This could perhaps be solved by fitting a downhaul to the head of the sail.

*　　　*　　　*

The catboat with wrap-around sails does have several advantages over a Bermudan-rig boat, the biggest being the ease of tacking without having to winch in a big genoa. This also results in there being no sheet winches to buy or maintain. Also, once more, the unstayed rig means no standing rigging to buy or maintain. On a good hull, the rig is close winded, and quite fast. Plenty good enough in this respect for cruising, and as Hoyt has all too regularly proven, the occasional bit of racing too.

There are definitely some shortcomings in raising, lowering and reefing. The problem of the wet sail sticking to the mast is hard to overcome with this type of sail. John Oakley, who handles Freedoms in the U.K., suggests that for a squall one may not need to reef at all. He says that by pinching up, until the lee side of the double sail flutters, the drive is almost halved. He suggests this as an alternative to reefing if the squall promises to be of only short duration. We have not had the opportunity to experience this for ourselves.

Should the sail be damaged, it becomes larger when you want to take it off the boat. With the wrap-around sail being doubled, it is in fact twice the effective area of the sail when set. This extra sail area also adds considerably to the cost of the sail, not only with the extra sailcloth that is needed, but also the extra labour involved in making the sail.

Catboats With Single-ply Sails

As the technology of building free-standing masts has improved, the diameter of such masts has been steadily decreasing. This has reduced the need to enclose the mast within the sail.

Several companies are using catboat rigs now with a single-ply sail that is held on to a mast track with slides, like many Bermudan-rigged sails, but set on small-diameter free-standing spars. For their single-ply sails, Freedom have gone to a fully battened sail, using flat carbon-fibre battens. The sail is attached to a mast track with slides, and uses a conventional boom with kicking strap.

The battens in the sail give most of the benefits that other fully battened sails do, although they are by no means as rigid as the battens in, say, a junk sail. They don't flog as much as a soft sail when allowed to feather into the wind, but neither do they lie as quietly as the junk sail does. The nature of the battens does cause some chafe at the forward end where they tend to bear on the mast as the sheet is eased, but they do help when it comes to reefing.

The sail is hoisted by a single-part halyard, and the boom is controlled by a multi-part sheet. The Freedoms are set up for reefing with a single pendant for each reef. Normally they can take two reefs in each sail. To reef, the halyard is slackened away, and the desired reefing pendant is pulled in. There are lazy jacks that gather the lowered sail and battens on top of the boom. Each reefing pendant runs from the cockpit to the mast, up through a block on the boom to the luff cringle, then back along the boom to pass through the leech cringle, in the manner that we described in the section on mainsails.

With this device, one pendant is sufficient for each reef.

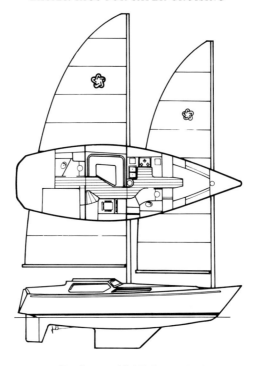

51. Freedom 39 with fully battened sails.

The battens and the lazy jacks hold the reefed sail onto the boom, so there is no need to tie in reef points. Likewise there is no need to go on deck to reef or unreef the sail.

Hinterhoeller Yachts, the Canadian company that build the popular range of Nonsuch catboats, also use a single-ply sail, but with short battens such as you might find on the equivalent-sized Bermudan sail. They have also elected to use a wishbone boom. Their reason for this is partly because all their boats have a single-masted rig, and on their Nonsuch 30, with a single sail of 520 square feet, a conventional boom would be some 26 feet long, which could well present problems for setting up a kicking strap efficiently. The wishbone boom, angled downwards, is self-vanging.

Their sail is set on slides that run on a conventional mast track. It is hoisted by a single-part halyard, and controlled by a multi-part sheet to the end of the wishbone. The wishbone remains in the 'hoisted' position all the time, but there is a line to the forward end, which they call the choker. This is used to push the wishbone aft, to flatten the sail for going to windward.

The single-ply soft sail does flap about somewhat if it is allowed to feather into the wind, or when tacking.

Beneath the wishbone is a cradle of line which virtually forms a hammock for the sail when it is lowered, or for the loose portion of the sail when it is reefed.

To reef the sail, the halyard is slackened away, and the

52. Nonsuch 30.

sail lowered the desired amount. There are separate reefing pendants for the luff and the leech for each reef, so once the halyard is slackened, the desired luff pendant, followed by the equivalent leech pendant, is pulled in. The choker, on the forward end of the wishbone is adjusted to set the outhaul tension on the sail. The reefed portion of the sail lies in its hammock, and there is no need to tie in reef points. Once more, with this rig reefing and unreefing can be accomplished without going on deck, provided all the control lines are led back to the cockpit.

Conclusions

With regard to the single-ply sail, the full-length battens certainly help to make a sail more docile, by reducing the amount that the sail will flap about. But to have full-length battens that press on to the mast track is to invite the risk of chafe which the soft sail would not be susceptible to.

Using a conventional boom and kicking strap tends to generate high loads in certain areas of the rig. A tight kicking strap and a powerful sheet to the centre of the boom can generate enormous forces on the boom, which will become a bending stress on the mast, at the gooseneck. If such a system is used, this strain must be allowed for, and the mast engineered accordingly. It is interesting that Freedom use a rather expensive carbon-fibre mast with the conventional boom and its induced high stresses, whereas Hinterhoeller use a rather less expensive spun aluminium lamp post with their wishbone rig, where the loads are more evenly spread. Probably both are adequate in their respective tasks. The aluminium lamp post, though, may not be up to the job if used with a conventional boom and a very tight kicking strap. This would lead one to expect that the wishbone rig, with a single-ply soft sail would be considerably cheaper than either the wrap-around sail, or the fully battened sail set on the conventional boom.

There does not seem to be any reason why one could not use a soft sail on a conventional boom, provided that one remembered the constraint of localised stress on the mast. Provided the problem of chafe can be overcome, the fully battened sail does have some merits.

The battens used in this type of fully battened sail are much lighter than those used on the junk rig and its developments. This is because the luff of the sail on this rig is supported by the mast and the sail is basically held in shape by the downward tension of the boom. By contrast, on the junk-type rigs the battens actually support the shape of the sail. As a result, these catboat sails, including the fully battened Freedom sails, are much lighter than the junk-type sails. This is a benefit when it comes to hoisting, but not when lowering the sail. Unless the sail slides are kept well lubricated, it is unlikely that the sail will come down on its own when the halyard is released, particularly in any kind of breeze. So lowering the sail may well require a trip on deck to pull the sail down unless a downhaul is fitted to its head.

So all three of the catboat-type rigs have their advantages and shortcomings. All offer easier sailhandling than a Bermudan-rigged boat so far as tacking is concerned. Each should be capable of being reefed as easily as the mainsail of any Bermudan-rigged boat. The catboats that we have seen have all been limited to a maximum of two reefs in each sail. This does not give one the flexibity of the junk-type rigs, where it is common to be able to reef five or more panels. On a two-masted cat-rigged boat, if she will still handle under one sail double-reefed, it is possible that the sail area can be sufficiently reduced for most gale conditions. However, on the single-sailed catboats, it is probable that even with the second reef tied in there will be times when less sail is needed. It may be possible to rig a third extra deep 'survival reef', or to bend on a trysail. Either are likely to mean a trip on deck just when we least want to be out there.

The single-masted cat rigs sometimes prove harder to manoeuvre in tight quarters than the two-masted version, or indeed, perhaps even than a conventional sloop. In a boat with a two-masted rig you can make the head pay off by oversheeting the foresail, which has somewhat the same effect as backing the jib on a sloop. This of course is not possible in a catboat with a single sail.

Also, on the single-masted rigs, Hoyt has found that a small headsail is really necessary to get the boat to go to windward. What he has adopted is a very small jib, set flying, with a small integral boom. This looks somewhat like half a wishbone, and is set in a pocket in the sail. It is angled downwards from part-way up the luff to the clew. By angling the boom downwards it keeps the leech of the sail fairly tight, and this reduces the load on the sheet, making the sail easy to be self-tacking. There is no doubt that this sail adds to the performance, though it also adds to the complication, but at least the rig is still self-tending, and you can still tack the boat without having to do any winching.

There is another rig that has been developed in North America, by Dick Carter, which he calls his Luna rig. This shares some of the characteristics of the Freedom rig, in that a single sail is set from each mast. However, in this case it is the mainsail that has gone, and a staysail is set in front of the mast. The French single-handed racing boat *Vendredi Treize* first brought this rig to prominence. She has three masts, and sets a single boomed staysail in front of each mast. With these staysails, the rig is self-tending, but in light weather she sets bigger overlapping staysails which have to be winched in after every tack.

For the rig to be self-tending when tacking, the sails cannot overlap the mast, so the size of the sails that can be set is limited by the height of the mast. On some of the other rigs, such as the junk, or the Freedom with a fully battened sail, sails with a large roach can be set. This substantially increases the area of the sail that can be set on a given mast.

Since the sails of the Luna rig are set on stays, which have to be kept tight, the mast has to be stayed at least as well as the mast on a conventional sloop or schooner. On such as the Freedom rig, one can have the choice of setting the sail on a free-standing mast, or if preferred, a fully stayed one. There is nothing to stop one from using a rig like the Freedoms on stayed spars should one wish to.

It seems to me that the Luna rig abandons the sails that are easier to handle, and retains those which are the more difficult to handle or to reef. Reefing on this type of rig is usually by roller reefing along the luff, in a similar manner to that used on Bermudan-rigged boats, and they face the same limitations that we have discussed earlier.

Whilst the Luna rig is an interesting concept, and exhibits a degree of original thought, I cannot see where it is better than the Freedom-type rig, and I do see in it certain inherent disadvantages.

So although many will see these various rigs as a progression forward from the junk rigs, and although they are certainly more efficient to windward than the basic junk rig, and less complicated than the Swing Wing or Gallant rigs, they do still have some limitations. However, for day sailing, coastal cruising with perhaps a bit of club racing thrown in, the cat rig does offer much easier handling than most Bermudan-rigged boats, and it will require less in the way of crew. For serious offshore cruising, though, I would personally select a rig that offered better reefing abilities, such as the junk rig or one of its derivatives.

For the more determined racers, who still want to get away from the requirements of a big crew, there are the rather more esoteric versions of the Freedom rig, involving rotating wing spars. Let's take a look now at this version, and some other high-tech. rigs.

7

Wing Masts and Solid Sails

There are those among us for whom speed is everything. Some of these folk have recognised the advantages of sail-handling from the cockpit, yet they still want to go as fast, or faster than the racing boys. For these people, development has concentrated on speed, often without regard to cost, while still trying to retain the easy handling features of some of the other rigs that we have looked at. In an effort to reduce the windage of the mast to an absolute minimum, various people have been using free-standing wing masts. These not only cause much less drag than a conventional mast, but, as we will see, they can actually generate lift, to augment that produced by the sails.

Wing Masts

Garry Hoyt has been experimenting with rotating wing masts on his Freedom boats for a number of years. His early experiments were with spars built by the Gougeon Brothers using their WEST system. Since then, Hoyt has gone to carbon fibre for his wing masts as well as for his free standard round masts, but the Gougeons have carried on building WEST wing spars.

The idea of using a rotating wing mast is to reduce the windage and turbulence caused by a round mast, and to try to get the best possible aerofoil shape for the mast/sail combination. The wing mast can be rotated so that it is at the optimum angle for reducing drag, or it can be rotated just a little less so that it generates lift.

It has become common practice to use fully battened sails in conjunction with the wing masts. The battens are usually much more flexible than those used with the junk rig, but they do still reduce the amount that the sail can flog, and they help in getting the sail to set to a proper aerofoil shape. They also definitely make life easier when it comes to reefing.

Hoyt's first experiments with a rotating wing mast were on a prototype of the now established Freedom 25. The prototype itself was rather more radical than the production boats turned out to be. It was somewhat lighter, built on the WEST system, and had a lifting ballasted dagger board. The early mast was also more extreme than those that eventually went into production. It was a composite WEST mast, beautifully built by the Gougeon Brothers. The mast was about four inches thick, and its chord, or width, was around two feet, giving the mast some sixty square feet of effective sail area, which is quite a lot of area on a very lightweight twenty-five footer. Indeed, in any kind of a breeze, the boat would sail and tack quite happily under mast alone.

Hoyt quickly decided that the boat would have to be detuned somewhat if it was going to be sold to the public, but we did have a couple of exciting sails on this boat while she was being tuned up ready for the annual Virgin Islands regattas. At the last moment, the Establishment would not let him race with the wing mast, so, undaunted, he borrowed the foremast and sail from a Freedom 30, and went racing anyway. The boat was a bit undercanvassed with this rig, so at every opportunity Hoyt was flying a large spinnaker, and when the jury-rigged backstay broke, the whole lot fell down. But back to the wing mast.

As we have said, the mast was able to rotate. On this first boat, the rotation was controlled by wires leading to a wheel mounted at the forward end of the cockpit. The degree of rotation of the mast could be changed at any time by turning the wheel. While learning to sail with this wing mast, Hoyt rigged a set of three 'Windex' wind direction indicators about five feet above the deck. Each 'Windex' was mounted on an arm about a foot long, which stuck out from the front of the mast. One was positioned directly in front of the mast, and one on each side at forty-five degrees to the central one. It was most interesting to watch these wind-direction indicators while the angle of rotation of the mast was altered. It was very easy to see at what point the mast was generating lift, and at what point it stalled.

If the mast was not rotated far enough, it would stall, and the leeward indicator would show poor air flow. If the mast was rotated too far, it would cause turbulence on the windward side of the mast, and the windward indicator would point almost at the mast. With the angle just right, the central indicator pointed in line with the axis of the mast, and the other two more or less pointed at the central one.

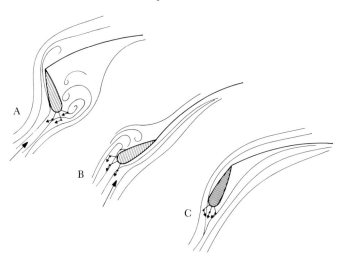

53. Air flow over a wing mast, A—over-rotated, B—under-rotated, C—generating lift.

Whilst it was very instructive to be able to alter the angle of rotation of the mast when sailing, it tended to be a little confusing to do. I found that to be steering with a tiller in one hand, and altering the angle of rotation of the mast with a wheel in the other hand was a bit like rubbing your stomach with one hand while patting your head with the other. It was also an added complication when tacking. It was very important that you did not forget to rotate the mast each tack, otherwise the sail pulled on the leeward side of the mast, making it bend alarmingly, and in a breeze it is possible that the mast could be damaged.

The following spring, Garry Hoyt returned to the Caribbean with the first production 25, and before the boat was even unloaded off the ship I was pestering him for a ride.

The boat was a little heavier than the prototype, and had a fixed keel, which at least stopped Hoyt from trying to pull the keel up while the boat was planing barely under control at fifteen or eighteen knots. He had given several crew members grey hair doing just that the previous year.

The wing mast was considerably smaller, and the system for rotating it had been simplified. Now, on the version that is being offered to the public, there is a lever about a foot long that sticks out from the after face of the mast, just below the boom. A length of line runs from the end of this lever to a cleat which is fastened beneath the boom. As the boom swings over, the line pulls on the lever, and the mast is automatically rotated. The forward push of the boom against the mast keeps it rotated, and the amount of slack in the line limits the degree of rotation. So once the line is set up to give the optimum degree of rotation, everything is automatic. We certainly found that this made the boat much easier to sail, as we no longer had to worry about the mast angle, and there was no danger of forgetting to rotate the mast when tacking.

When Hoyt put the wing mast into production, as we

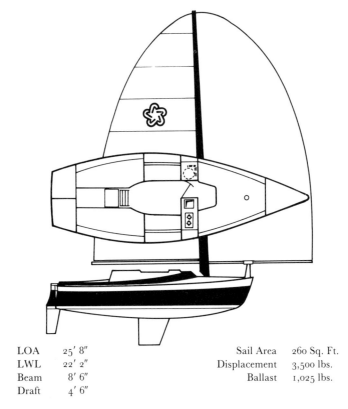

LOA	25′ 8″	Sail Area	260 Sq. Ft.
LWL	22′ 2″	Displacement	3,500 lbs.
Beam	8′ 6″	Ballast	1,025 lbs.
Draft	4′ 6″		

54. Freedom 25 with wing mast.

mentioned, he made it rather smaller than the prototype, and changed from WEST construction to carbon fibre. The production mast for the Freedom 25 has a chord of something under eighteen inches, and it is amazingly thin, around three inches at the thickest point. It looks more like a knife blade than a wing. We were curious to see how much it would bend in a breeze, and got a surprise when we sailed the boat for the first time on a windy day.

Going to windward in a fairly strong breeze, I went forward to look up the mast and saw that it was actually bending to windward. Because of the rotation of the mast, and the pull of the mainsheet along the leech of the sail, the top of the mast was definitely hooked slightly to windward, which was not what I had expected to see. With the sail sheeted in hard, there was surprisingly little flexing of the rig, as the little boat jumped happily from wave to wave.

Tacking is simplicity itself: just put the tiller over and round she comes. As the boom swings over it pulls the mast round ready for the new tack, and the full-length battens keep the sails from flogging. There is no winching to be done, and the whole process is silent. The Freedom 25 is so light and responsive, one would expect it to be very manoeuvrable, and it certainly is. On a heavier boat, the single-masted rig might not prove so good, and a two-masted rig, either a ketch or schooner, would be more manoeuvrable when short tacking, or if trying to bear away in a hurry.

The sail is attached to the mast by a boltrope which is pulled up an aluminium extrusion bonded into the after face of the mast. Hoisting the sail with its light battens was easy enough, but it really needed somebody on deck to help feed the luff of the sail into the extrusion. Likewise when shaking out a reef, there was sometimes a reluctance for the sail to feed itself back into the extrusion. A roller feeding mechanism would help more than somewhat.

Reefing was straightforward and easily done from the cockpit. The system for reefing is exactly the same as we described for the fully battened sails on the standard Freedom rig. Suffice it to say here that the system worked well—two reefs could be put in without going on deck at all. The lazy jacks and the full-length battens hold the reefed part of the sail quite happily on top of the boom, without the need to tie in any reef points.

How well does the rig perform? To windward, the prototype could just about hold a well-sailed J 24. The production boat, unless burdened down with an excessive amount of cruising gear, is only a little slower. Both boats that we sailed were fitted with Hoyt's innovative 'Gun-mount' spinnaker, and using this on a close reach in most conditions the boat is at least as fast as the J 24. So she is certainly a slippery little boat, and even with the 'Gun-mount' spinnaker in operation, which we will look at in detail in the next chapter, she can be easily and safely sailed with a crew of two. Indeed, because of the appeal of this, a series of races has been initiated for the Freedom 21 and 25 where the crew is limited to two, and must be one of each sex. The rules further stipulate that nobody can leave the cockpit, except briefly, to attach a boom vang. Sounds like my kind of racing—I never could understand the appeal of spending every Sunday afternoon perched up on the weather sidedeck of a yacht, while it thrashed up and down the coast.

We have not yet had the chance to compare the performance of a Freedom with a wing spar directly to one with a round spar. But Gougeon Brothers, who fitted one of their wing spars to a Nonsuch 30, reported a 'considerable' improvement in the wing spar compared to the standard unstayed round spar on all points of sailing, but particularly to windward.

Gougeons have also successfully fitted a ketch rig with wing spars to a Herreshoff-designed hull, which had previously sailed with round carbon-fibre spars. Again they noted a general increase in performance, but especially when going to windward, as is perhaps to be expected.

They have also built a number of wing spars for racing multihulls, including the late Phil Weld's *Rogue Wave*. The French are likewise building ever bigger wing spars for their fleet of big racing multihulls. However, because of the multihull's initial stability, which can put sudden shock loads on the rig when a gust hits, and the wide platform available to

55. Nonsuch 30 catboat *Purr-fect Dazy* with Gougeon Brothers' Wing mast.

stay the rig to, these wing masts all tend to be stayed. Also, as these boats are primarily concerned with speed, all other factors—from cost through handling to safety—appear to be secondary considerations.

*   *   *

123

The wing spars do offer an increase in performance over the equivalent unstayed round mast, but at a considerably increased cost. Whether the one is worth the other is largely a question involving the depth of one's pocket. It would appear that with modern materials there is no problem about getting a wing spar to stand unsupported, but I feel that for open-water cruising, the round spar has perhaps a greater safety margin built in and might prove easier to handle in extreme conditions.

For racing, the wing-spar rig offers performance close to any other racing boat, yet retains the virtues of no sail changing, easy reefing from the cockpit, and no need to sign up lots of deck apes to wind winches. There is definitely a certain appeal there. Unfortunately, the racing Establishment do not seem to welcome innovation, and it is not likely that a wing-masted boat is going to be allowed to race without severe rating penalties. Racing for these boats is likely to be restricted to three types of race: the long-distance racing, where boats are not handicapped, but only divided into classes by length; the less serious racing, governed by locally modified rating rules; and class racing with a particular design, such as Hoyt is promoting for the Freedoms.

For a cruising boat, there is one drawback to the rig. Since the mast is a very efficient aerofoil in itself, there is a marked tendency for the boat to sail about at her anchor. The easiest way round this problem, under most conditions, is to anchor by the stern, when the mast will be far enough away from the effective bows of the boat to reduce its effect to a minimum. However, I would not like to be anchored by the stern in a strong wind, in an exposed anchorage. Clearly some other solution would have to be found before undertaking serious cruising with the rig. It may well be possible to leave the mast free to rotate, and set a small riding sail on the boom to make the mast weathercock into the wind so that it could not generate lift to get the boat sailing.

This problem is perhaps not so great on a boat with two masts. Possibly if each mast was locked at a slight angle, on opposite tacks as it were, the boat would stabilise and not sail around too much at anchor.

Another difficulty might be encountered when trying to manoeuvre the boat under power in a strong wind and a confined space. As the boat changes her heading with respect to the wind, the effect of the wind on the rig will vary dramatically.

At sea, there is the potential of being able to make to windward, or indeed to sail on any point under mast alone, in strong winds. If the sail is damaged, it should be possible to keep the boat under control while repairs are effected. In extreme conditions, it is possible to set the mast at a very fine angle of attack to the wind, to reduce the drive generated as required. When running before the wind in really heavy weather, if the mast is 'sheeted in' amidships, the windage will be reduced to a minimum, much less than on a conventional rig, or indeed on an unstayed round mast. What is effectively a solid wing sail may well prove to be an asset when trying to sail under extreme conditions, if only because it saves you from going on deck to rig a storm jib or trysail when the going gets tough. One of the big French racing multihulls is reputed to have done twenty-six knots under wing mast alone, during a transatlantic race in heavy conditions. I am not sure that this is the sort of performance we should be looking for on a cruising boat!

Primarily though, I see this rig as ideal for somebody who still enjoys a bit of racing, but has got tired of the deck apes drinking his beer, and who would like to see where he is going, rather than gaze at a row of oilskin-clad bottoms lining the weather deck.

For those people who are interested in the 'high-tech.' rigs, there are the solid wing rigs, that do not have any sails in the conventional sense.

Solid Sails

Over the years one keeps hearing the sails of a boat likened to an aircraft's wings, and there have been various attempts to replace the boat's soft sails with solid wings. The 'C' class catamaran that races for the Little America's Cup is one type of boat that sometimes sports very sophisticated solid wings. These are very high-tech. and very expensive devices, where the camber of the aerofoil can be altered and precisely controlled. In this context they are striving for the maximum possible speed from a given 'sail' area. There is scant regard to cost, and little regard to ease of handling, either afloat or ashore. To think of such a rig for cruising would be like buying Mother a formula one racing car to go to the supermarket.

However, solid sails have recently attracted another group of people who are looking for what may be the easiest possible rig to handle, perhaps by crew who know nothing about sailing. These are the people who are looking for ways to make sailing commercial vessels a paying proposition once again.

Japanese, American and British companies, amongst others, are working on this project, and for commercial ships, the systems that show the most promise right now are the solid wingsails. Although much of the work being done is concentrated upon large commercial ships, particularly tankers, some of the technology may well spin off into the yachting world. Let's take just a brief look at one of these wingsail systems, and see what perhaps the future holds in store for us.

The most advanced wingsail system at the moment is that built by John Walker at Walker Wingsail Systems. Some twenty years ago John Walker started experimenting with wingsails and built the research boat *Planesail*. Since then, he has refined his thinking and built the present wingsailed *Flyer*. *Flyer* is a hydrofoil-stabilised trimaran, that sets a single wingsail above an aircraft-style cockpit. John Walker boasts that the only piece of rope on the boat is for the anchor.

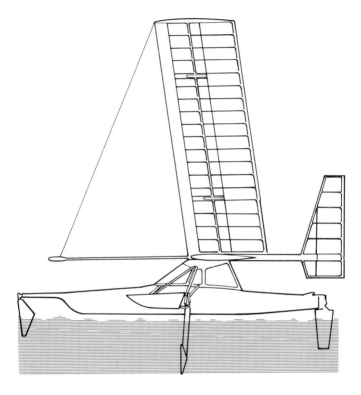

56. John Walker's *Flyer*.

The aerofoil itself has been the subject of extensive wind-tunnel testing. The result is an aerofoil that is in three sections, that can be articulated to alter the camber to the optimum for any given windspeed, and can be reversed for tacking. The section is quite thick, with a well rounded leading edge to reduce the tendency to stall. There are slots between the sections of the aerofoil to enhance the flow of air over the surface. In operation it looks very much like the wing of a big jet with flaps extended ready for landing.

This section is actually so efficient that it generates a coefficient of lift a little over twice that generated by the rig of a twelve-metre yacht when going to windward. With the wind astern, the wingsail is deliberately stalled, and the resulting thrust is about twice that of a square rigger also on a dead run. So there is little doubt that the wingsail has the potential to generate more thrust than any other type of sail.

With the Walker system, the wingsail is mounted on a freely rotating mast, and is normally kept weathercocking into the wind by a tail stabiliser. It has been found in practice that the wingsail can rotate at up to thirty degrees per second in response to windshifts. This means that at anchor, with the rig weathercocking, there is little problem of the boat trying to sail about on her anchor.

On *Flyer*'s sail there are just two controls. One control adjusts the camber of the wingsail, and the other alters the angle of the tail fin. As the angle of the tail is altered, this causes the wing to rotate on its axis, and so presents the wing at the correct angle to generate lift. Once under way, minor course changes and windshifts are compensated for automatically by the tail swinging the rig to the optimum angle.

Any required adjustments can be made from inside *Flyer*'s enclosed cockpit. On the commercial system it is envisaged that these controls will be handled by a computer. The computer will receive continuous inputs giving the wind direction and strength. When the desired course and speed is fed in, it will set the wingsails to generate the best lift, then instruct the engine to make up the difference in required thrust to attain the desired speed.

The commercial wingsails are basically three of *Flyer*'s sails set side by side. The triplane arrangement gives the best results when comparing the space required and thrust available. Walker has drawings available for a variety of craft using his sail sets, from thirty-metre passenger-carrying ferries up to quite large tankers.

*   *   *

Walker has tended to concentrate on the big-ship end of the market, but the success of *Flyer* has shown that the rig is feasible for smaller vessels. Potentially it offers fingertip control from inside the boat. There is no need to change or indeed reef the sails. John Walker feels that reefing a sail is analogous to removing cylinders from a car engine every time you stop at a traffic light! He claims that the rig can be sufficiently depowered by altering the camber and the angle of attack to prevent any problems in strong winds. Certainly to date *Flyer* has survived intact in quite strong winds. Perhaps this is the way of the future, but as far as the average weekend sailor is concerned, it is probably a long way in the future. Maybe, though, if the price of oil increases, such a rig might well appeal to the motorboat brigade, and if they used the computer control concept, they would not even have to learn how to sail!

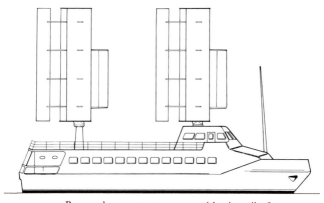

57. Proposed 32-metre catamaran with wingsails, for
passenger ferry service.

8

Setting Lightweather and Downwind Sails

Most boats will benefit from adding a bit more sail in very light conditions, or when sailing off the wind in light to moderate conditions. Although these are the conditions when we don't mind working on deck too much, handling these big sails can and does still cause problems. This is particularly true for a family crew that has perhaps left the sail up too long, and is now faced with getting the thing down. It is all too easy to be lulled into a false sense of security while running downwind on a nice sunny day. You only realise just how much the wind has freshened when you come to get the sail down, and suddenly you are struggling.

I have a very healthy respect for big lightweather sails ever since getting caught out in just this way. We were crossing the Atlantic on a hundred-foot schooner, running happily down the Trade Winds, averaging better than two hundred miles a day. One particularly nice morning, more for something to do rather than out of any sense of trying to hurry, we set the gollywobbler. This was an enormous sail, getting on for ten thousand square feet, running from the stemhead, via the top of the foremast, to the top of the mainmast, and down almost to the stern.

We got it up and set alright, and it added a couple of knots to the speed of the boat. The weather stayed sunny, and since we were running with the breeze nobody noticed how much it had freshened until it was too late. The boat was getting a bit hard to steer, so we decided to get the sail off her before dark. While we were still plucking up the courage to start, a small tear appeared in the foot of the sail. That was the end of that sail. Before anybody could move, there was a rushing sound, and the whole sail just disintegrated before our eyes. All that was left for us to lower were the boltropes and the tablings. We counted ourselves lucky that it was only the sail that got destroyed. Although the results may not be quite so spectacular on a smaller boat, it is all too often during the lowering of lightweather sails that problems occur.

There are some easy ways of setting these light sails, and even more importantly, of getting them down without having a whole team of people eager to break their fingernails wrestling with a flogging sail. Let's look at a few of them.

Taming the Spinnaker
The most sophisticated system that we have seen is that used for setting the spinnaker on the Freedoms. Indeed, this spinnaker-handling system is perhaps the most innovative thing that Garry Hoyt has come up with, and it really does make the spinnaker a sail to consider when cruising shorthanded. The system is patented, and at the moment it is

58. Freedom 25 with spinnaker set.

59. Garry Hoyt's Freedom 21 with spinnaker set.

available only on Freedom yachts, but there is no reason why the system could not be made on a one-off basis, for one's personal use, and used on almost any boat.

The secret of the system is what Hoyt calls his 'Gunmount'. This is a pivoting sleeve, through which the spinnaker pole can slide, and which is mounted on top of a reinforced bow pulpit. The pivoting sleeve allows the pole to rotate horizontally, but prevents either end of the pole from rising.

Hoyt has things arranged so that everything can be done from the cockpit. This has resulted in a profusion of control lines, but if they are colour-coded and led through marked stoppers, it is all quite easy to use in practice. We will run through the setting process in detail, and describe each control line as we come to it.

132

When not in use the pole is normally stowed along the top of one guard rail, pulled back as far as it will go in the sleeve. There are a pair of control lines that run forward to the pivot, and out, one to each end of the pole. Using these two lines, it is possible to move the pole forward until it is centred in the pivot sleeve. These lines can then be cleated off; they will not be needed again until it is time to stow the pole.

Next the pole is swung round until it is approximately across the wind. The lines to do this lead from each end of the pole directly to the cockpit. Hoyt has given these lines the rather un-nautical name of reins, but it is easy to see the analogy.

The spinnaker is normally stowed in the fabric tube that lies on deck. The two clews of the sail are drawn from the mouth of the tube out to the ends of the pole by pulling on the sheets, which run forward to the pivot and out through a block on either end of the pole. Once both clews are pulled all the way out, the sheets can be cleated off; they will not be touched again until the spinnaker is stowed.

Now the sail can be hoisted. This is done by pulling on the halyard. As the sail goes up, it will fill quite early on in the hoisting, so it is necessary to keep a turn or two around the winch, so that it doesn't fill suddenly and take charge. It will probably be necessary to use the winch to finish off the last bit of hoisting. As the sail is being hoisted, the tail of the halyard vanishes down the after end of the tube, and is attached to the centre of the spinnaker to become a down-haul when dropping the sail.

All that remains now is to trim the pole at the best angle to the wind, using the reins. There is no need to take these round a winch, since almost all the thrust of the pole is taken by the 'Gun-mount'. Even in strong winds, it is easy to hold the reins by hand, and alter the trim of the pole at will. Even when sailing on Hoyt's overcanvassed lightweight prototype

Freedom 25 on a screaming reach, it was possible to sit in the companionway with a 'rein' in each white-knuckled hand, and keep the spinnaker perfectly trimmed, even if the rest of the boat was barely under control. Amazing!

Gybing the spinnaker is very straightforward. It is just a case of altering the trim of the pole slightly as the course changes. There is no need to touch the other controls, and of course, no need to go on deck at all. If a fairly flat-cut spinnaker is used, it can be carried on quite a close reach, again being easily trimmed and controlled by the reins, still without needing to use winches.

Dropping the sail is also very easy. It can be done on a reach, but it is easiest if running down wind. To drop the sail, the halyard is released, and as the sail comes down, the tail of the halyard is pulled. As mentioned, the tail is fastened to the centre of the spinnaker, and it pulls the spinnaker back down into the tube quicker than it takes to describe the process. Once the spinnaker is basically down, the other control lines can be used to put everything away. The sheets are cast off, and the spinnaker pulled completely into the tube. The reins are used to point the pole fore and aft, and the other control lines pull the pole back into the boat.

With this system, not only is it possible to set and drop the spinnaker from the cockpit, without any of the foredeck antics that a spinnaker normally demands, but when the sail is up, it is much more manageable than any conventional spinnaker. There is no danger of the pole suddenly rearing up to the sky, nor any chance of the sail getting away from the pole in a gybe. To use the current idiom, it makes the spinnaker 'user-friendly'.

For those who feel confident about controlling a conventional spinnaker once it is up, but who worry about getting the thing up and down, there is another way. That is using a fabric tube that pulls down over the sail. Since I have never felt comfortable using a conventionally poled out spinnaker on a short-handed cruising boat, let's look at this system when used with a poleless, or so-called cruising, spinnaker.

Controlling a Poleless or Cruising Spinnaker

The last few years have seen a profusion of cruising spinnakers offered for sale, all with cute names such as Genniker, Cruising Chute, Thrasher, or the more esoteric Multi-Purpose Sail. Give or take a few subtleties of cut, these are all the same basic sail: a sail that is set flying, as opposed to being hanked onto a stay, but one corner of the sail is tacked down to the deck rather than being held out on the end of a pole, like a true spinnaker. The fact that one corner of the sail is attached more or less directly to the boat makes the sail much easier to handle, and less prone to go into some of the wild oscillations for which spinnakers are renowned. They can still cause some interesting moments when being set or dropped. Let's look at how they can be kept under control.

For many years, racing dinghies have set and dropped their spinnakers by using a fabric tube which runs along the deck, or just below the deck, similar to Hoyt's. There is no real reason why such a system could not be used on a larger boat for setting and recovering a cruising spinnaker. There would be some deck-work involved, as the tube would have to be laid out and the sheet reeved according to which tack the boat was on. Since the sail is not symmetrical, it has effectively to be turned inside out when changing tacks. The other problem with this type of system is that there is a tendency for the sail to fill perhaps before you might wish it to do so. At best this means having to winch the halyard up for the last bit, or at worst, the halyard gets away and runs out through someone's hands, and gives a nasty rope burn.

A better system is one that allows you to get the sail all the way up, and the halyard cleated off, before the sail has a chance to fill. The racing boys fasten their spinnakers into a long sausage shape, using either cotton or elastic bands to stop the sail. The sausage of sail can be hoisted, and when ready, and hopefully not before, a tug on the sheets breaks the stops, and the sail fills. We could resort to this method for setting our cruising spinnaker, and it would work well, but it would not help when it came time to get the sail down again.

To get their sails down, the racers will usually let go the tack of their spinnaker, and drag the clew into the cockpit and pull the sail in under the boom. This again is a possible solution for us. The tack of the cruising spinnaker is usually set on an adjustable pendant, which goes through a block near the stemhead. Releasing this tack pendant, and pulling the sail into the cockpit by the sheet is often easier than trying to quell acres of sailcloth that is enveloping you on the foredeck when you try to drop the sail by releasing the sheet. It is particularly easy to bring the sail in under the boom if the boat is more or less on a dead run while trying to perform the manoeuvre.

A much better way is to use one of the devices that pull a tube down over the sail. Several variations on the theme are available commercially, with names such as Squeezer or Snuffer, which describe their function quite well. Whatever the name, the device consists of a long tube of fabric and a smooth circular rigid mouth. The sail is pulled up into the tube, with the head secured to the top and the mouth of the tube enclosing the bottom of the sail. A light line runs from the mouth assembly, up inside the fabric tube through a small block at the head, and back down to the deck. The tail of this line is attached to the outside of the mouth assembly ready to use as a downhaul when dousing the sail.

In use, the whole sausage containing the sail is brought up onto the deck, the tack pendant attached to the stemhead, the sheet reeved through its blocks, and the halyard attached to the top of the tube. While it is being hoisted there is no chance of the sail filling prematurely, since it is totally enclosed by the fabric tube. Once the halyard is secured, and the slack taken out of the sheet, the light line is pulled to raise the mouth of the tube up the sail. The fabric tube collapses above the mouth assembly as it slides up the sail, and the emerging sail fills beneath it. While the sail is set, the tube remains in place concertinaed at the head of the sail.

When it comes time to lower the sail, the sheet is freed, and the tail of the light line that leads to the mouth assembly is pulled down. The mouth assembly slides down over the sail, and the tube engulfs the sail until just the sausage of bundled up sail is left. This can be lowered easily and safely to the deck at leisure, with no flapping, flogging or broken fingernails.

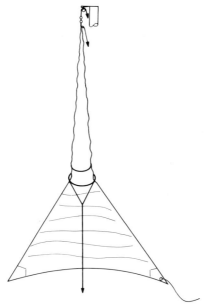

60. Spinnaker squeezer in action.

Conclusions

For the spinnaker really to become a safe and easy sail for short-handed cruising, it is probably necessary to use a system similar to Hoyt's 'Gun-mount'.

Under most conditions, except on a dead run, a cruising spinnaker is almost as efficient. Using a tube system for setting and dousing the sail, the cruising spinnaker is entirely feasible for a short-handed crew to handle.

If using such a system on a rig that is unstayed, great care must be exercised, as a sail of this sort concentrates most of its force on the masthead, rather than spreading the load evenly through the mast. In any sort of breeze, it will probably require the use of a running backstay, to take some of the load off the mast. If the sail is only a lightweather sail, and no running backstay is fitted, then it is a good idea to use a piece of fishing line for the tack pendant. This way, if the boat is caught by a sudden gust, the fishing line will break, and release the pressure from the sail before there is any risk of damaging the mast.

Either way, a lightweight offwind sail can add interest and speed to the passage, and need not take a lot of effort or a big crew to handle it. We have found that, using a tube system, one person can set and safely douse sails up to about a thousand square feet. Without the tube, I am much happier to see the big sails stay in their bags.

9

The Construction of
Unstayed Masts

The technology used in the construction of unstayed masts has advanced quite rapidly over the past few years, and it is likely to continue to do so for the next few. As in the rigs themselves, there are high-tech. and low-tech. methods of construction. Some methods require a huge outlay for equipment, so they are worth considering only for a series production. Other ways require little in the way of equipment, but are quite labour-intensive. These ways might suit the one-off builder or even the home builder.

Let's look at some of the ways, and consider the choice of material, which comes down to wood, metal, or reinforced plastics of various sorts.

Wooden Masts
The original unstayed mast was undoubtedly a solid wooden spar. Trees have been standing for thousands of years under often impressive spreads of leaves, in strong winds, and when they do fall down, it is quite rare for them to snap, it is much more common for them to be uprooted. The simplest possible unstayed mast is basically a tree of the right dimensions.

We used 'grown' masts in our own junk-rigged boat very successfully for three years. The only problem that we ever had with them was in the tropics—it was a problem to keep them oiled to stop them drying out and splitting. The pundits say that these splits, or shakes, do not weaken the mast provided that they run along the grain and do not spiral.

Ours showed no tendency to spiral, but they were a little off-putting, so when we were offered some of Garry Hoyt's reject experimental masts, we decided to change. The masts we got were, he said, too strong, and hence too heavy for his boat. They were much lighter than our trees, would not need regular oiling, and the price was right, so they sounded perfect for us.

The trees we originally used were Norway Spruce which we obtained from the local forest, courtesy of a helpful forester. We selected two trees that were straight, as near as we could guess the right sizes, and that were growing in a dense part of the forest. This was important, as such trees will grow slower, giving a greater number of growth rings per inch and hence greater strength than a tree of quicker growth. Also the closeness of the other trees reduces the number of branches that the tree will grow, which correspondingly reduces the number of knots in the finished mast.

The most exciting part of the whole operation was transporting the two forty-foot trees on a twenty-foot truck, right through the middle of town to my parents' house, where we were leaving them to season. The only time that we really caused a good-sized traffic jam was when the front of the trees went the wrong side of a set of traffic lights, while we were trying to make a left turn. While my long-suffering parents held up the traffic outside their house, we and a group of friends muscled the trees into their garden, where they stayed for almost a year.

We got conflicting advice on how best to season the trees, and right or wrong, this is what we did, and it seemed to work for us, since these masts are still sailing, almost eight years later, now in another boat.

The first job we did was to strip off the bark, since this is much easier to do when the tree is first cut, than if it is left until later. We had to have the trees cut in late summer, so we weren't worried about them drying out too fast in a British autumn. The experts claim that for choice you should cut the trees in late autumn, as there is then less sap in the trees, so they will be lighter to handle, and will dry out quicker.

The next job was to block them up clear of the ground in a sheltered spot where they did not get too much wind, which might cause them to dry out too quickly and perhaps split. It is very important to block them up straight and level, otherwise you will be sailing with a bent mast.

We left them like that for six months, just rotating them every couple of months to let the whole surface get a chance at what sun there was. After that time, they began to show some signs of drying out. Thankfully they had already lost a considerable amount of weight, I guessed at least a third, but perhaps a little more. Initially we had been horrified when we felt the weight of the two trees, and wondered if our little boat was going to be able to carry them. They were to the size suggested by Jock McLeod, so we carried on hoping that it would all turn out alright. Now that they had lost some weight, we started to feel a little more confident. As soon as they started showing signs of splitting, we started oiling them weekly with raw linseed oil, thinned down with pure turpentine—an expensive mixture, but we had been assured that that was the best thing to use, and it certainly stopped the masts from splitting excessively, yet still allowed them to continue to lose weight.

At the one-year mark, much to the annoyance of my parents' neighbours, we took an electric plane to the trees, and planed off the bumps to turn them into masts. We did not follow the traditional practice of using an oversize tree, and cutting it square, then octagonal and finally round. Instead we chose trees that were almost the correct size, and planed off the bumps, which is better for unstayed spars, as the outer ring of sap wood makes the resultant mast significantly stiffer. Had we followed the traditional practice, we would have removed all the sapwood.

Once sailing, we kept the masts slushed down with a mixture of linseed oil and Vaseline. A messy job, but necessary in the tropics (we have been living in the Caribbean) to prevent them from splitting too much.

As to what size of mast to use, we were guided by the recommendations set forth by Jock McLeod in his junk-rig design folios. There are several books that quote sizes, but the information from Jock is the most comprehensive that we have seen, and for anybody considering building an unstayed rig the purchase of his design folios would be a worthwhile investment if only for the sections on masts.

It is possible to build up hollow wooden masts for free standing rigs, and such a mast would obviously save some weight aloft, compared to a solid one. The traditional way to build up hollow wooden spars is to scarf together long pieces of timber, then build the mast in two halves. A groove is cut in each half to make what will become the hollow centre, then the two halves of the mast are glued together. This obviously requires a high degree of woodworking skill, and we never really considered this method feasible with our rather limited abilities.

61. Section through a traditional hollow wooden mast.

A couple of years after we had made our masts, we learned of a much easier and quicker way, that exploits the properties of a modern epoxy glue. The method was pioneered by Barry Noble of Bristol, and he has developed a technique for building hollow wooden spars of almost any size that does not require fantastic woodworking skills.

Basically he uses square sections of timber, and cuts a right-angled notch into one face of each piece. The corner of the next piece fits into the notch, and if the process is repeated, you end up with an octagonal mast. The corners can be planed off afterwards to make it round.

Provided the joints are staggered, it is not necessary to scarf the lengths of wood together. Each piece can simply be butted to the next, with little loss in strength. A circular saw can easily be set up to cut the right-angled notch in each piece of timber.

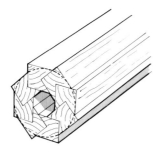

62. Showing how the corners of square sections fit into the notches to make an octagonal mast, which is planed down to make a round mast.

63. Section through an oval mast built the same way.

143

By tapering each square piece of timber, it is easy to produce a tapered mast, or to vary the wall thickness along the length of the mast. If the width of the two side pieces is increased, an oval section can be produced.

If the mast is put together with epoxy glue, and the inside and outside surfaces of the mast are treated with epoxy resin after the WEST style, then such a mast should last well, and not suffer from drying out like a solid one does. This is probably the easiest way for an amateur to build a hollow spar, and had I learned about it before our trip to the forest, I think I would have had a go at building our masts this way.

Metal Masts
For the type and size of boat that we are interested in, steel masts are too heavy, and the space-age metals like Titanium are too expensive, so our choice is effectively limited to various alloys of aluminium.

A tapered mast not only looks better, but it saves quite a lot of weight aloft. Towards the top of the mast the stresses are usually less, so the diameter and the wall thickness can both be reduced, to save weight where it most counts. Metal mast sections are extruded, and usually come out as long straight tubes, with a constant wall thickness.

There are three ways that a tapered mast can be made from an alloy extrusion. It is possible to cut long thin wedges out from the section, squeeze the pieces together and weld up the cuts.

This system is very often used on masts in a stayed rig. For an unstayed mast there are some limitations. Welding aluminium alloys is a science all to itself, and often such welding will change the properties of the metal, so that stress points or areas of local weakness get built into the mast—not a good start for a new mast that is expected to support itself without any rigging.

A method often used for making tapered things such as

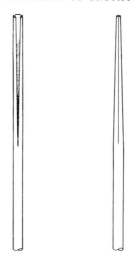

64. Tapered aluminium mast made by cutting out tapered pieces and then welding.

65. Mast section being spun-tapered. As the mast rotates, the rollers squeeze the section smaller, and move along the mast to give it the required taper.

aluminium flagpoles and lamp posts also starts off with a constant-section extrusion, which is cut to the desired length. The area which wants tapering is put into a machine, which squeezes the section with a set of rollers while it is being turned at high speed within the machine. Such a spar is said to be spun-tapered.

145

This process can produce a nicely tapered and smooth section, without the local stresses that welding causes. Usually spun-tapered masts can be recognised by the characteristic circular patterns around the mast where it has been tapered.

The only real drawback to a spun-tapered mast is that as the section of the mast is squeezed smaller, the amount of metal in that section stays the same, which makes for increased wall thickness. This means that in the area where you would be looking for a decrease in wall thickness, to save weight aloft, you are actually getting an increase. The weight per foot of the mast section is the same along its length, where ideally it should decrease substantially towards the top.

The other thing to be wary of with such sections is that they are often produced for non-marine needs, such as flag-poles and lamp posts. There are many different types of aluminium alloy, some of which are stronger than others, and some of which are less prone to corrosion than others. You should make sure that the mast-maker knows what alloy is used in the mast, and ensure that it is indeed suitable for use as a mast.

The third type of aluminium mast is extruded with the desired taper built in. Such sections are extruded on complicated machines that have a die which changes diameter while the metal is being extruded through it. The diameter and the wall thickness can be controlled, so unnecessary weight can be eliminated. Such masts can be distinguished from spun-tapered ones by the extrusion marks that run along the length, rather than around it. These masts are likely to cost a little more, because of the high cost of the machinery involved, but since they are being produced specifically as masts, it is likely that they will be made from a marine grade of alloy, which the flagpoles may not be.

Masts Made From Reinforced Plastics

It is with masts made from reinforced plastics that development is taking place most rapidly, and where the future would appear to lie. Even at the present time, the choices are almost bewildering. We are faced with a choice not only of reinforcing material and resin, but there are several different techniques for actually making the mast. All these choices affect not only the ease of manufacture and cost, but also the final properties of the mast itself.

Let's work through the choices of materials and processes in turn, and we will find that some of the choices in selection will be made for us. Cost obviously varies with the choice of materials, but also varies with the technique chosen. Some techniques require super-sophisticated machinery, so obviously would not be suitable for a home builder to make a single mast. Once we decide whether we are looking for the ultimate in performance, or the best type of mast for series production, or if we want to build a mast for ourselves, the choices will become fewer.

Reinforcing Materials. The three main types of reinforcing material are carbon fibre, Kevlar and glass.

Carbon fibre is the stiffest and strongest of all the fibres, and perhaps not surprisingly, the most expensive. It is made of carbon which is about ninety-five per cent pure. It is lighter than glass and it is very strong, both when in tension and in compression. This is very important in an unstayed mast because as the mast bends, one side is being stretched, that is, it is in tension, while the other side is being squashed, or is in compression. Carbon fibre is readily obtainable, and is quite easy to use. The only difficulty that I have found in using it compared to glass is that the fibres are so shiny it is difficult to make sure that they have been thoroughly wetted out with resin. In most commercial processes, the carbon fibres are impregnated with resin by machine to overcome this, and to ensure uniformity.

Kevlar is an aramid fibre which is lighter than carbon fibre, and although it is considerably stiffer than glass, it is not as stiff as carbon fibre. Its biggest shortcomings are its poor compressive strength, and its high cost. It is not often used in the manufacture of masts.

Most of us are at least somewhat familiar with glass when used as a reinforcing fibre with a plastic resin. This is an advantage in itself, as most users are already familiar with its properties, and feel comfortable using it. There are several different types of glass which are used to make a variety of fibres, cloths and mats.

The glass that is most often used in boat-building is called 'E' glass. However, 'S' glass is almost twice as strong, and is only a little more expensive. It is similar to 'E' glass to work, and so when glass is used in a mast, it is better to use 'S' glass wherever possible.

The Choice of Resins. Whatever fibre, or mixture of reinforcing fibres, is chosen, they must be bonded together with a resin to form the structural unit. The various resins exhibit different properties, and their cost varies quite dramatically.

The usual resin used in boat-building is a polyester resin. Whilst polyester resins can and have been used for making masts, they are far from ideal. There are much stronger resins that are just as easy to handle, and polyester resins shrink as they cure. In boat-building, where usually the parts are moulded inside a female mould, shrinkage does not cause any difficulties, indeed it can even be a help in getting the part out of the mould. However, when we look at the techniques for making masts, we will find that most techniques use a male mould, where the mast is laid up around a mandrel, or former. Here, if the part shrinks on curing, it can render it impossible to remove from the mould.

So although polyester is sometimes used by the amateur mast builder, often for no better reason than that is what he has, it is not often used commercially.

Epoxy resin is the strongest of the readily available resins. It is not too easy to use for laminating, as it is rather toxic, and can cause skin problems in some people. However it does not shrink on curing, and assuming that you are not one of the people who react badly to epoxy, it is feasible to use it for a one-off job. This will produce the strongest possible mast, but because of the complications, it is not often used for production masts.

The resin that is most often used for production masts is a vinylester resin. It handles much like polyester, but it is stronger and more elastic, though not quite as strong as epoxy. The biggest plus is that it does not shrink on curing, so it is feasible to use male moulding techniques without fear of getting the part stuck onto the mould. Even for the one-off mast builder, it is probably worth seeking out a supply of vinylester resin for the project.

Techniques for Laminating Masts from Reinforced Plastics. As we already mentioned, most boat builders use a female mould, and laminate the part up inside the mould, and this technique is possible for making a mast. Obviously one cannot reach very far up inside the mould, so it must be made in two halves. If the mast is round or oval, it would be feasible to use one mould for both halves of the mast. It is possible to vary the taper along the length of the mast by the shape of the mould, and it is very easy to change the wall thickness by adding extra layers where the stress is concentrated, for example at the partners, where the mast goes through the deck.

Each half of the mast is laid up in the mould, to perhaps half of its desired thickness, then the two halves are removed, and bonded together. Extra layers are laminated around the outside of the mast to build up the finished thickness, and to ensure that the two halves stay together.

Working with an open mould like this allows local reinforcement where fittings will be fastened, and also allows quite complicated shapes to be formed. This would be the easiest way to mould a wing mast for example.

A rather more sophisticated mould was used for some of the early round masts, and could perhaps be used for wing masts too. This type of mould is hinged to allow access for laminating. Once the laminating is complete, an inflatable bladder is laid inside, and the mould closed. The bladder is then inflated, and pushes the laminate against the mould while it cures. Once cured, the bladder is deflated and the mould opened to release the part. Apart from the cost of the mould and the bladder, each of which can be used only for one type of mast, such a system requires some pretty sophisticated moulding techniques. All the laminating must be completed, the mould closed and the bladder inflated before any of the laminate starts to cure. This technique does not appear to be used much now, having largely been replaced by newer technology and easier methods.

The most commonly used of the high-tech. methods is a technique called filament winding, which involves a rather complicated machine that lays down continuous lengths of impregnated fibres onto a moving mandrel.

The filaments are drawn off reels through a resin bath and fed onto the mandrel, which rotates and moves backwards and forwards in a predetermined pattern, so building up the required layers. Once all the required layers have been applied, the laminate is allowed to cure, and the completed mast is jacked off the mandrel.

This system is well suited to computer control, and masts with a high degree of uniformity can be produced once the machine is set up. Almost any size of mast can be made—all that is required is the relatively inexpensive mandrel for

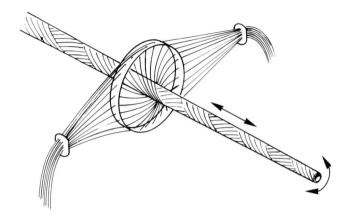

66. Filament-winding machine. Fibres are drawn through a resin bath and wound onto the mandrel, which rotates in alternate directions and moves back and forth.

each size and taper of mast that is built.

The drawbacks are that the initial cost of the equipment is very high, so to be economical, a lot of masts must be made. These machines cannot usually lay the filaments exactly along the length of the mast, the mandrel must rotate a little, to wrap the filaments at least partially round the mandrel to keep them in place while curing. This reduces the stiffness of the mast, which must be made up for in increased wall thickness or diameter. When a solid mandrel is used, the mast almost has to have a uniform taper along the entire length, otherwise when it comes to jacking the mast off the mandrel, sticking may occur. With a constant taper, as soon as the mast is moved a little, it is completely free from the mandrel.

A somewhat less sophisticated technique is also used with a rotating mandrel, where alternating layers are wound around the circumference of the mast and laid along its length. The machine winds the layers of carbon fibre or glass round the mast, and layers of uni-directional rovings, again of carbon or glass, are laid by hand along the length of the mast.

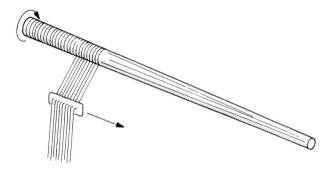

67. Mast being made with alternating layers round and along the mast. Filaments are drawn through a resin bath, and the guide moves along while the mandrel rotates. Longitudinal layers are applied by hand.

This technique is much more labour-intensive, so it is harder to ensure uniformity of the product. However, the initial investment is much less, in fact the whole process can be done by hand without using any sort of machine. It is also much easier to mix different types of filaments, for example, all the longitudinal fibres could be carbon, and the fibres that run round the mast could be glass, which would make the mast cheaper. The main longitudinal stiffening fibres can be laid exactly along the axis of the mast, which will make it stiffer, and it is easy to increase the wall thickness by adding extra layers in any particularly highly stressed areas. This is the way the masts that we presently have in our boat were made.

For the builder of a one-off mast this technique can be modified to use a disposable male mould, to save the cost of a proper metal mandrel. Jack Manners-Spencer has built

152

several masts for his Gallant rig with just such a technique.

He uses a five-inch-diameter alloy tube for a former, which is rather longer than the finished mast will be. The tube is supported where the ends of the mast will be, and counterweights are hung on the ends to reduce the effects of sag in the tube. He then makes up a series of foam circles to the inside diameter of the mast. These are threaded onto the alloy tube former and spaced at about eighteen-inch intervals. On the Gallant boats the diameter of the mast is constant, but there is no reason why a tapered mast could not be made this way. All that is needed is to vary the diameter of the foam circles.

The next stage is to cover the foam circles with cardboard to give a smooth surface on which to laminate. The first and last layers of laminate should be done round the circumference of the mast, and the bulk of the other layers should be along the length of the mast.

Once the laminating is finished and the mast is cured, the foam formers can be broken out with a long bar, and the former removed. This technique is labour-intensive, but it requires little in the way of equipment, and also has the advantages that any taper can be built, the wall thickness can be varied at will, and the layers can be orientated in the most advantageous directions.

Before we leave the subject of masts made from reinforced plastics, a word of warning about the use of carbon fibre. Carbon conducts electricity very well, and it behaves as a very noble metal if one considers its effects on electrolysis. Only gold and silver are considered more noble than carbon, and this can lead to electrolysis of fittings. An aluminium track fastened with aluminium rivulets will last an extremely short time, and even stainless steel fastenings will suffer. As far as possible fittings should be glued onto the mast, or well-insulated on bedding compound, and fastened with oversized fastenings. One tends to think of masts being made of plastics as being inert, but in fact they are definitely not. However, taking these precautions into account, a mast made of reinforced plastics should give many years of low maintenance.

Conclusions

For a low-tech. rig, such as the junk rig, solid grown spars are the cheapest and easiest to build for the amateur. For a production mast, either carbon fibre or purpose-built aluminium masts are very satisfactory.

A determined amateur should be able to build either a laminated wooden mast, or a composite plastic mast, and the choice should perhaps be determined by where his skills lie. But the sensible amateur builder might elect to concentrate on building the boat and buy a ready-made aluminium or carbon fibre mast.

Appendix

USEFUL NAMES AND ADDRESSES

Design Services Aerosystems. Jock McLeod. Sunbird Yachts.
Mainsail Reefing Systems Hood Sailmakers.
Headsail Roller Reefing Systems Hood Sailmakers. South Coast Rod Rigging.
Boats Aerosystems. Freedom Yachts. Hinterhoeller Yachts. Newbridge Boats. Sunbird Yachts.
Junk Sails W. G. Lucas.
Masts Freedom Yachts. Gougeon Brothers. Hood Sailmakers. Kenyon. Needlespar.
Wingsails Walker Wingsails.
Reference Junk Rig Association.

Addresses

Aerosystems Jack Manners-Spencer, Kelham, Dock Lane, Beaulieu, Brockenhurst, Hants. so4 7YH, UK (Gallant-rigged boats to 45 feet: design service and parts kits.)

Freedom Yachts International Ltd. Portsmouth Road, Lowford, Southampton, Hants., UK (Cat-rigged boats from 21 to 70 feet, with wing mast option on smaller boats. Market carbon fibre masts made by Tillotson Pearson.)

Freedom Yachts International Inc. 49 Americas Cup Avenue, Newport, R.I. 02840, USA (See above.)

Gougeon Brothers P.O. Box x908, Bay City, Mich. 48707, USA (WEST system wing masts.)

Hinterhoeller Yachts Ltd. 8 Keefer Road, St Catherine's, Ontario L2M 7N9, Canada (Builders of the Nonsuch range of catboats.)

Hood Sailmakers Ltd. Bath Road, Lymington, Hants. so4 9RW, UK (Stowaway masts and booms. Stowaway in-mast reefing systems. Seafurl roller-reefing systems.)

Hood Sailmakers Inc. Box 928, Little Harbour Way, Marblehead, Mass. 01945, USA (See above.)

Junk Rig Association Secretary: P. Weigall, 16 Fairfield Road, Bosham, Chichester, West Sussex PO18 8JH, UK (Issues newsletter covering junk rig and variations.)

Kenyon Masts P.O. Box 308, Guildford, Ct. 06437, USA (Carbon fibre masts.)

W. G. Lucas & Son Ltd. 42 Broad Street, Portsmouth, Hants. PO1 2JF, UK (Makes more junk sails than anybody outside of China!)

Jock McLeod Hawk Hill, Rosemarkie, by Fortrose, Ross-shire, Scotland, UK (Design folios for junk rig, including specifications for unstayed masts.)

Needlespar Ltd. 207 Warsash Road, Warsash, Southampton, Hants. so3 6JE, UK (Tapered aluminium extruded masts.)

Newbridge Boats Ltd. Church Street, Bridport, Dorset, UK (Junk-rigged boats, especially up to 23 feet.)

South Coast Rod Rigging Sparkes Boatyard Co. Ltd., Sandy Point, Hayling Island, Hants. PO11 9SR, UK (Manual and power roller-reefing systems.)

Sunbird Yachts Ltd. 373 Hunts Pond Road, Titchfield, Fareham, Hants. PO14 4PB, UK (Junk-rigged and Swing Wing boats to 32 feet. Design service, and parts kits.)

Walker Wingsail Systems Ltd. The Point, Hamble, Hants. so3 5PG, UK (Builders of *Flyer* and developing wingsail systems.)

Index